THE
REAL
APOCALYPSE

Solving the End-Times Bible Prophecy Puzzle

Daniel Baker

ISBN 978-1-0980-7045-8 (paperback)
ISBN 978-1-0980-8288-8 (hardcover)
ISBN 978-1-0980-7046-5 (digital)

Christian Faith Publishing, Inc.
832 Park Avenue
Meadville, PA 16335
www.christianfaithpublishing.com

Printed in the United States of America

For my children and all those who are looking for
the blessed hope and the appearing of the glory
of our great God and Savior, Christ Jesus

CONTENTS

PREFACE

Over the last century, some two hundred million human beings have perished due to the ravages of war and oppression. That is more death, misery, and suffering than all the conflicts of the previous one thousand years. In just the last forty years, something even more unconscionable has happened. One billion six hundred thousand unborn babies have been slaughtered in the womb worldwide.

During this period, something amazing took place. Jews from all over the world began migrating back to the land of Palestine, and in 1949, Israel was formally declared a nation again. Against all odds, after nearly two thousand years of extinction, Israel was reborn.

It is not surprising that people are interested in Bible prophecy today more than ever. Yes, people throughout the centuries have wondered about the end of the world. But until the twentieth century, conflicts and disasters were local and regional, not worldwide. And Israel did not exist.

Today, with the coronavirus calamity, its associated looming worldwide economic collapse, the fomenting riots and anarchy, the growing unbridled lawlessness, and the rapid eradication of individual freedoms, Jesus's rebuke of the Jews in the Gospel of Luke seems more relevant than ever: "You know how to analyze the appearance of the earth and the sky, but why do you not analyze this present time?"

INTRODUCTION

Therefore, prepare your minds for
action, keep sober in spirit, fix your hope
completely on the grace to be brought to
you at the apocalypse of Jesus Christ.
—1 Peter 1:13

Apocalypse—the end of the world by every catastrophe imaginable. Thanks in large part to Hollywood, that is usually what comes to mind when you hear the word *apocalypse*—bad news! I would agree that it is not good news. That is, if you are not a Christian. But for Christians, the message that the Day of the Lord is near, the Apocalypse, is great news!

In actuality, the word *apocalypse* comes from the Greek word *apokalupsis*, which means "revelation," "manifestation," or "disclosure." Every time it is used in Scripture with reference to Jesus, it means His appearance, revelation, or coming for believers.

It is wonderful news for Christians, and we should crave to know about it. The more you know, the more encouraged you become, the greater your reverence and awe of the Living God, and the more passionate the expectation of His coming.

I have found that as I keep this knowledge fresh in my daily life, the stronger my sanctification from the corruption of the world is. I think this is what Peter was getting at about when he wrote the following:

Since all these things are to be destroyed in this
way, what sort of people ought you to be in holy
conduct and godliness, looking for and hasten-

9

ing the coming of the day of God on account of
which the heavens will be destroyed by burning,
and the elements will melt with intense heat! (2
Peter 3:11–12)

As we consider the coming events foretold in the Word, the
effect is a powerful binder on our perspective. It keeps it where it
needs to be. And in a way, it hastens the coming of the day of God,
or Day of the Lord. Our mind-set toward time is affected. Time
becomes more compressed.

Christians are being told from various quarters of the faith to
prepare for the end of the world. *Apocalypse* is a dreadful word for
them. They tell us to "stock up supplies," "prepare for survival," and
"prepare to go through the wrath of God!" How can that be good
news? It is not, but what the Bible teaches is.

This book is an anthology of articles that I have written over
the past three years. My goal was to organize a book that explained
future events foretold in the Bible in a way that was enjoyable and
easy to read as well as theologically sound. As the great Christian
author A.W. Tozer said, "Some books claiming to be exhaustive are
only exhausting to read."

This is not a systematic walk through the Bible. It is not a technical research manuscript. It is a series of articles that I have written
and published about different pieces of the Bible-prophecy puzzle.
I believe that as you read about each piece, the entire picture will
unfold before you. I think you will find this a fresh way to approach
Bible prophecy.

It is also not a book that attempts to link every current event to
some prophecy in Revelation. There is a plethora of material like this
in the marketplace, and frankly, I think most of it is futile speculation.

I am not a pastor or a theologian. I am not a graduate from sem-
inary. What I am is an ardent student of the Scriptures. I have been
doggedly studying the Bible, specifically Bible prophecy, for nearly
twenty years. And I have been blessed to have been able to teach in
my church.

I have always been interested in Bible prophecy. I became a Christian forty-one years ago when I was in college. God used Bible prophecy to reach me. I had a sense that we were living in unique times even then, and He made the most of that sense to draw me to Him as He exploited my desire to understand what was happening in the world.

It was about twenty years ago when I decided I would find out with certainty what the Bible teaches about the future. I reasoned that if God had it written, then there must be a lot that could be known with certainty. I found this to be the case but for a few exceptions. There are some things that will only be understood on an as-needed basis.

There are three parts to this book. Part 1 endeavors to explain what the Bible teaches leading up to the seven-year Tribulation, which precedes the physical return of Jesus Christ to earth. The second part will focus on the events during the Tribulation and after the return of Jesus to earth. Part 3 is supplemental, an important bonus if you will. You will find answers to these questions:

- What was Jesus's real mission when He first came?
- What was Peter's vision on the roof really about?
- Is a believer's salvation secure?
- What really happened between David and Goliath?
- What is the truth behind the Tower of Babel?

While there are many different positions on Bible prophecy, there is only one truth, one position. God did not intend for His Word to have multiple meanings for His agenda for the future. There is one plan and one plan only. If you know how to study the Bible, it is amazing what you can extract. Unfortunately, I believe this is one of the failings of Christian churches, at least in America. They do not teach believers how to properly study the Bible.

There is a lot of what I call junk theology in the marketplace. Many ministers and so-called scholars publish material that just does not hold up under sound exegesis. I call it junk theology, for instance, when someone takes a verse from one book and another verse from another passage and thinks that because they sound somewhat similar, then they must be talking about the same thing. And then a theological position is created. However, when closely examined, the context of each is completely different, and they have nothing to do with each other.

I have learned from some tremendous Bible scholars as I read their books and papers. I learned that there are four main pillars of sound interpretation. Those pillars are context, grammar, historicity, and reading the Bible literally unless it expressly indicates a metaphor or analogy. I have concluded that, most of the time, if you can figure out the context, you have figured out 99 percent of what you need to know. In my opinion, with a little effort, understanding God's agenda for the future is not as complicated as it may seem. And you don't have to be a Bible scholar. In addition to gaining a clear understanding of future events, I hope that this book will equip you for better interpretation of the Bible.

If you are new to Bible prophecy, I think you will enjoy this book for its unique topical approach. If you are a veteran of prophecy, I think you may find some surprises. Either way, my hope is that by the time you have read each chapter, you will have a clearer understanding of what is about to take place in heaven and on earth.

What you will discover as you read, if you are not aware of it already, is that there is a pattern or sequence of events that will take place before Jesus Christ returns to earth. You will especially find this sequence in Daniel 9, Matthew 24, 1 Thessalonians 5, 2 Thessalonians 2, and Revelation. This sequence is consistent throughout Scripture.

Once you understand this sequence, navigating end-times Bible prophecy becomes much easier. As I stated in the preface, each article is a piece of the puzzle. Do not become frustrated because one article does not explain everything or leaves some things unanswered. Be patient and continue reading. I am confident that everything will come together for you as you do.

PART 1

I wrote this book for the church, but it is also for every person who is searching for spiritual answers to the tumults of our time and the future.

I assume that most people reading this will be born-again, Holy Spirit-filled Christians. And most who read this probably understand that there will be a period on earth prior to the physical return of Jesus Christ where God will pour out His wrath on the world. This time is called the Tribulation in the Bible. Many misappropriate the word *apocalypse* for this period. Most also know that this period of judgment is seven years in duration. It is sometimes referred to as the seventieth week of Daniel.

Where the biggest debate exists is what takes place prior to the Tribulation. The Bible teaches that the church or the body of believers will be evacuated from the earth. This is known as the Rapture, or Departure. The word *rapture* is not in the Bible, but *departure* is. I will show you in this first part that the Bible guarantees the body of Christ will not experience the wrath of God during the Tribulation.

If you are one who holds the position that the church will go through some or all the Tribulation, I urge you to have an open mind and consider the points I make in this book. You may not have heard some of them before. Let's start with a brief explanation of the Tribulation.

1
The Seventieth Week of Daniel

Seventy weeks have been decreed for your people
and your holy city, to finish the transgression, to
make an end of sin, to make atonement for iniquity, to bring in everlasting righteousness, to seal
up vision and prophecy and to anoint the most
holy place.

So you are to know and discern that from
the issuing of a decree to restore and rebuild
Jerusalem until Messiah the Prince, there will
be seven weeks and sixty-two weeks; it will be
built again, with plaza and moat, even in times
of distress.

Then after the sixty-two weeks, the Messiah
will be cut off and have nothing, and the people
of the prince who is to come will destroy the city
and the sanctuary. And it's end will come with a
flood; even to the end there will be war; desola-
tions are determined.

And he will make a firm covenant with the
many for one week, but in the middle of the week
he will put a stop to sacrifice and grain offering;
and on the wing of abominations will come
one who makes desolate, even until a complete
destruction, one that is decreed, is poured out on
the one who makes desolate. (Dan. 9:24–27)

The phrase "seventieth week of Daniel" comes from the passage above. Seventy weeks of time were decreed by God for, among other things, atonement of Israel's sins. Sixty-nine of those weeks have been completed. There is one more week to complete.

Seventy weeks represent seventy periods of seven years. Between the time of Moses and Nebuchadnezzar—over eight hundred years— Israel violated God's command 490 times to give the land a Sabbath rest. If you divide 490 by 7, you get 70.

In Daniel 9, the archangel Gabriel comes to Daniel to explain what is going to happen to Israel because of its transgressions. He tells Daniel that from the decree to rebuild the plaza and the moat of Jerusalem, there would be 69 weeks, or 483 years, until the Messiah would be "cut off and have nothing."

At the time of Gabriel's conversation with Daniel, much of Judah was in exile in Babylon, including Daniel himself. After Persia conquered Babylon, King Cyrus freed the Jews to go back to Israel. Not only did Cyrus free the Jews but he also decreed that they rebuild the temple of Solomon (Ezra 1:1–4).

But that was not the decree Gabriel was talking about. He was talking about the decree to repair the plaza and moat. In 444 BC, Artaxerxes, who succeeded Cyrus, decreed that the Jews could rebuild the plaza and moat of Jerusalem (Neh. 2).

Sixty-nine weeks, or 483 years later, Jesus was crucified. He was "cut off and had nothing." He did not receive His kingdom on earth. This partially fulfilled the prophecy.

That leaves the seventieth week, the final week. Daniel 9:27 explains the final seven years as the Tribulation. It will begin with a treaty or agreement between the Antichrist and Israel. I believe the agreement will, in part, allow the Jews to rebuild the temple and begin sacrificing. I will explain more about this later in the book.

In the middle of the week, or three and a half years, the Antichrist will stop the sacrifices and desecrate the temple by entering the holy of holies and declare himself to be God Almighty (Dan. 9:27, Matt. 24:15, and 2 Thess. 2:4).

At the end of the seven years, Armageddon will take place, and Jesus will return to earth, and the Antichrist will be destroyed. This is how the seventieth week is arrived at.

The 70th Week of Daniel

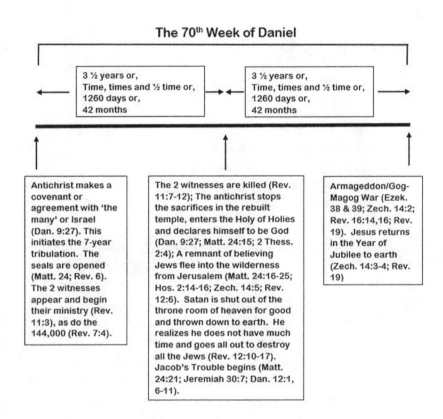

| 3 ½ years or, Time, times and ½ time or, 1260 days or, 42 months | 3 ½ years or, Time, times and ½ time or, 1260 days or, 42 months |

| Antichrist makes a covenant or agreement with 'the many' or Israel (Dan. 9:27). This initiates the 7-year tribulation. The seals are opened (Matt. 24; Rev. 6). The 2 witnesses appear and begin their ministry (Rev. 11:3), as do the 144,000 (Rev. 7:4). | The 2 witnesses are killed (Rev. 11:7-12); The antichrist stops the sacrifices in the rebuilt temple, enters the Holy of Holies and declares himself to be God (Dan. 9:27; Matt. 24:15; 2 Thess. 2:4); A remnant of believing Jews flee into the wilderness from Jerusalem (Matt. 24:16-25; Hos. 2:14-16; Zech. 14:5; Rev. 12:6). Satan is shut out of the throne room of heaven for good and thrown down to earth. He realizes he does not have much time and goes all out to destroy all the Jews (Rev. 12:10-17). Jacob's Trouble begins (Matt. 24:21; Jeremiah 30:7; Dan. 12:1, 6-11). | Armageddon/Gog-Magog War (Ezek. 38 & 39; Zech. 14:2; Rev. 16:14,16; Rev. 19). Jesus returns in the Year of Jubilee to earth (Zech. 14:3-4; Rev. 19) |

That was a quick snapshot of the doctrine of the seven-year Tribulation. For a much more comprehensive study of this, I would recommend two books on Daniel. One is by Renald Showers titled *The Most High God*. The other is by John Walvoord titled simply *Daniel*.

2

Michael the Restrainer?

> And you know what restrains him now, so that in his time he may be revealed. For the mystery of lawlessness is already at work; only he who now restrains will do so until he is taken out of the way. (2 Thess. 2:6–7)

The next two chapters will address the identity of the restrainer in 2 Thessalonians 2. In my opinion, this piece of the prophecy puzzle is the single most important determining factor for the timing of the Rapture. There are plenty of others, but this cinches it.

Recently, I watched a video online by a pastor by the name of Dean Odle. He was teaching on a subject I was interested in hearing about. At the outset of his teaching, he laid out four principles of proper Bible interpretation. In a nutshell, the principles he laid out were reading the Bible literally unless a passage is metaphorical or allegorical, context, grammar, and historicity. I was encouraged to hear this from the pulpit because my experience tells me that this is a glaring weakness in the church. Most Christians simply do not know how to properly study the Bible.

At one point in his message, he said that he believed that the archangel Michael was the restrainer in 2 Thessalonians 2. His basis for this position was Daniel 12:1.

> Now at that time, Michael, the great prince who stands guard over the sons of your people, will arise. And there will be a time of distress such as

never occurred since there was a nation until that time; and at that time your people, everyone who is found written in the book, will be rescued.

The pastor said that Michael is going to "arise" and get out of the way and by doing so will allow God's wrath to pour out on the earth. According to him, as I understood it, this will happen after the sixth trumpet of Revelations, and this is when the Antichrist is revealed.

Notwithstanding the fact that the Antichrist is revealed long before the sixth trumpet (he is revealed at least at the beginning of the seventieth week of Daniel when he spearheads a treaty or covenant with Israel [Dan. 9:27]), the pastor violated all the principles of interpretation that he said he believed were essential to understanding Scripture. I wrote him the following email.

Dear Pastor Odle,

I watched the video of your message on the coming great deception.

One of the things I appreciated was your walk-thru of how to study the scriptures accurately. Most churches do not teach their members how to "rightly divide" the word, which is a genuine shame.

Along those lines of good hermeneutics that you spoke of, I wanted to challenge you on something you said, namely that the restrainer is Michael the archangel. You cited Daniel 12 and I believe you are in error in your interpretation of that passage. The context is key. What you did is what many Christians do, which is put the Church (and in the case of your teaching, the Church, and the rest of the world) into passages where it does not belong.

In Daniel 12, the context is referring to Daniel's people. Michael is standing guard over them as it says in vs. 1.

Michael is not standing guard over the whole world. What Michael is there to do is protect the righteous Jews—whose names are written in the book. The verse says they will be rescued. This verse is referring to Jacob's Trouble, the Great Tribulation, which is the 2nd half of the tribulation (little t) or 2nd half of the 70th week of Daniel (Dan. 9). The passage says it will last a time, times, and a half of time, which we know is 3 ½ years (Dan. 12:7).

Notice it says it will be a time such as never occurred for a <u>nation</u>—not the world. We know that a remnant will be rescued. Jews will flee into the Judean hills east of Jerusalem the moment the antichrist takes his seat in the Holy of Holies and be protected there for the 3 ½ years (cf. Matthew 24:15–22 and Rev. 12:6). Jesus speaks of the same thing regarding the last 3 ½ years in Matthew 24 with respect to Jacobs Trouble/Distress.

Michael is charged with protecting Daniels people whose names are written in the book— they will be rescued. The people in this passage are Daniel's people—-the Jews. Rev. 12 says that during the last 3 ½ years Satan is going to try to wipe out Israel and the Jews, but he will fail. Michael is not the restrainer in 2nd Thessalonians—the context in Daniel 12 denies that. That is NOT Michaels job. I would love to hear your response.

Thanks, and blessings to you.

Unfortunately, I never got a response. In summary, Michael is not charged with protecting the world; he is charged with watching over Israel and the Jews. He is not the restrainer.

3
Who or What Is the Restrainer?

> And you know what restrains him now, so that in
> his time he may be revealed. For the mystery of
> lawlessness is already at work; only he who now
> restrains will do so until he is taken out of the
> way. (2 Thess. 2:6–7)

In my previous article, I dispensed of the notion that the restrainer is
the archangel Michael as many incorrectly believe. Daniel 12:1 is the
only Scripture reference that I know of that is used to support that
contention. So who or what is the restrainer?

Of all the other possibilities, the only one that makes sense,
considering all the requirements of restraining the evil one, is the
Holy Spirit. Here are the ways the Holy Spirit fulfills the role:

- The Holy Spirit is God and is therefore more powerful
  than Satan.
- The Holy Spirit operates in the spiritual realm as does
  Satan.
- The Holy Spirit dwells in His church, which is His body.
  The church is the salt of the earth or preservative (Matt.
  5:13).
- The whole world lies under the power of the evil one (1
  John 5:19), yet the gates of hades will not prevail against
  the church where the Holy Spirit dwells (Matt. 16:18).
- In 2 Thessalonians 2:6–7, Paul uses the words *what* and *he*
  to describe the restrainer, which rules out Rome or govern-

ment. The "what" is the power of the Holy Spirit, and the "He" is the person of the Holy Spirit.

Again, Michael has been ruled out. It is not that person, nor is it Caesar or any other political figure or earthly government because they can neither transcend the centuries nor have worldwide power.

No other possibility makes as much sense. That being the case, the only way the restrainer can be removed is if the church is removed. This supports a pre-Tribulation Rapture. Why?

The Tribulation, otherwise known as the seventieth week of Daniel, begins when a covenant or agreement is forged with Israel facilitated by the Antichrist (Dan. 9:27). Therefore, the Antichrist is revealed at minimum at the time of the treaty/covenant, which means he is revealed at the beginning of the Tribulation, not in the middle.

If the Holy Spirit is the restrainer, then the removal of the church happens before the Antichrist is revealed. The Tribulation cannot start until the Antichrist is revealed because the Antichrist will enact the covenant or treaty with Israel that begins the Tribulation, and everyone will know who the Antichrist is at that time.

This is really all you need to know with certainty: the Rapture will take place before the Tribulation. But there is much more.

4

Times and Epochs

> Now as to the times and the epochs, brethren, you have no need of anything to be written to you. For you yourselves know full well that the day of the Lord will come just like a thief in the night. While they are saying, "Peace and safety!", then destruction will come upon them suddenly like birth pangs upon a woman with child; and they shall not escape. But you, brethren are not in darkness, that the day should overtake you like a thief. (1 Thess. 5:1–4)

There is a lot to unpack in these four verses. Here, we see that sequence or pattern I spoke about in the preface. Paul summarizes what is going to happen regarding

- the church and the Rapture,
- those who do not know the Lord at the time of the Rapture, and
- the beginning of the Tribulation.

First, we must determine what Paul is referring to in verse 1. To find out, we must look back to the preceding verses. Chapter 5 verse 1 is referring to when the Rapture will take place. Look at chapter 4 verses 15–17. Paul describes what is going to happen at the Rapture, how things are going to happen, and the sequence of the events. Here is the passage.

For this we say to you by the word of the Lord, that we who are alive, and remain until the coming of the Lord, shall not precede those who have fallen asleep.

For the Lord Himself will descend from heaven with a shout, with the voice of the archangel, and with the trumpet of God; and the dead in Christ shall rise first.

Then we who are alive and remain shall be caught up together with them in the clouds to meet the Lord in the air, and thus we shall always be with the Lord.

In chapter 5 verse 1, Paul tells the Thessalonians that they have no need of him writing anything to them about the timing of what he just talked about in the verses mentioned above. The reason Paul says this is because he had most certainly explained everything in extensive detail when he was with them in person (1 Thess. 2:1, 2 Thess. 2:5).

The believers in the church in Thessalonica were terribly concerned about their brethren who had died. They were grieving for them, and Paul comforted them by explaining that they would rise from the dead and meet the Lord in the air at the Rapture, just as those who were alive at that time would also meet the Lord in the air (1 Cor. 15:51–52).

So in chapter 5 verse 1, he is referring to the Rapture. In verse 2, he says it will come like a thief in the night. The Day of the Lord is the Rapture, but it is also much more.

"Day of the Lord" is an idiom. It means the time when the judgment of Yahweh is going to come to earth. It is referring to the seventieth week of Daniel or the seven-year Tribulation that precedes the physical return of the Son of David to earth. It is a term that represents the beginning day (Rapture—thief in the night), all the events of judgment and wrath throughout the period of the Tribulation, and the very day that Jesus sets foot on the Mount of Olives.

It is signaled by the Rapture, however, and that is what Paul is specifically referring to in chapter 5 verse 2. The Rapture will happen like a thief in the night. No one knows when the thief will come, but when it does, it is the beginning period of what will become the most terrible ever on earth. It is the opening bell of the Day of the Lord. Chapter 5 verse 3 describes what happens next.

Peace and safety

> While they are saying, "Peace and safety!", then destruction will come upon them suddenly like birth pangs upon a woman with child; and they shall not escape. (5:3)

The first thing we need to determine in this verse is who "they" are. To find the antecedent, we must go back to chapter 4 verse 5. In the context, Paul is talking about "the Gentiles who do not know God."

> Not in lustful passion, like the Gentiles who do not know God. (4:5)

You can't really say he is talking about the outsiders in chapter 4 verse 12 because the Greek word there essentially means "whoever."

> So that you may behave properly toward outsiders [whoever] and not be in any need. (4:12)

So unbelievers would be the general definition of "they" in chapter 5 verse 2—"Gentiles who do not know God." They will be rejoicing that the world has finally achieved peace and safety. It is the culmination of godless humanism on earth, a false utopia.

We know that when the church is evacuated, the Holy Spirit will be removed and that the Antichrist will be revealed. When the Holy Spirit is removed and perhaps as many as a billion people disappear, then literally all hell will break loose on earth. It will undoubtedly be a time of chaos and economic collapse on a scale the world has never seen. But it is NOT the tribulation yet. This is the stage that the Antichrist will step up on, and these are the events that will allow him to ascend to total world power.

In 2 Thessalonians 2:8–10, Paul says he will come with "all power, signs and wonders and every deception of wickedness." The Antichrist will miraculously stabilize all the upheaval, violence, and economic chaos. He is going to usher in a golden age, and he will be viewed as the savior of the world.

How long this golden age of peace and prosperity lasts, we do not know. It could last months, maybe longer. So for a time, the world will be dwelling in peace and safety (physical and economic) such as never before. This is what Paul is saying in chapter 5 verse 3. Then the Tribulation will begin, suddenly like birth pangs.

At first, it sounds like an oxymoron or paradox—suddenly out of the blue and yet gradually. It describes precisely the same thing Jesus taught in Matthew 24. The Tribulation comes on like birth pangs. The judgments, or wrath of God, will be poured out in increasing intensity and frequency over the seven-year period. Just as in child-birth, it is the first pang that comes suddenly and surprisingly.

This first pang is the first seal described in Revelation 6:1. It will happen after the Antichrist has facilitated some grand agreement with Israel, which will be the technical beginning of the seven years (Dan. 9:27). When the first seal is opened, the peace on earth will end. And it only gets worse from there (see the chapter on birth pangs).

Remember "they" in verse 5:1? Well, Paul says they will not escape. Why? Because there is no rescue for those who are not rap-tured. The church escapes. That's what the word *delivers* (Greek *ruomai*) means in 1 Thessalonians 1:10.

> [We] wait for His Son from the heavens, whom
> He raised from the dead, that is Jesus, who
> DELIVERS us from the wrath to come.

The word *ruomai* literally means "to be rescued by physically dragging someone out of the way." Every believer who is alive when the thief in the night comes will be dragged up to meet Him in the sky and out of the way of the wrath that is coming. But the remaining earth dwellers will not escape.

The Thief is coming

Since the Antichrist is revealed at that time, this means the church has been evacuated prior to the seven-year Tribulation. Remember, the Antichrist is not revealed until the restrainer (Holy Spirit) is taken out of the way. When the church is removed, the Holy Spirit is taken out of the way, and the Antichrist will be revealed. The church will thus be raptured prior to the seven-year Tribulation.

5
The Great Falling Away of the Church

> Let no one in any way deceive you, for it will
> not come unless the apostasy comes first, and the
> man of lawlessness is revealed, the son of destruc-
> tion. (2 Thess. 2:3)

Most evangelical Christians believe there will be a great falling away
or rejection of Christ by the church before the Rapture happens.
However, there is no worldwide falling away from the faith by the
church prophesied in the Bible. That is not what this verse is saying.

The "it" in the verse above is the Day of the Lord. That is what
Paul says in the preceding verse: "That you may not be quickly
shaken from your composure or be disturbed either by a spirit or a
message or a letter as if from us, to the effect that the day of the Lord
has come."

Chapter 2 verse 3 is saying the Day of the Lord will not
come unless the apostasy comes first. When Paul wrote this, the
Thessalonians thought they were in the Day of the Lord, or the
judgment of the world, i.e., Tribulation. Most Christians understand
this passage to say that the apostasy is the body of Christ in general,
falling away from or rejecting the faith. It is understood to mean
that there will be a mass rejection of Jesus by the church before the
Tribulation period begins, otherwise known as the seventieth week
of Daniel.

The Day of the Lord will come as a thief in the night as Paul
said in 1 Thessalonians 5:2, which indicates the Rapture will take
place before the Tribulation. Therefore, according to this incorrect

scenario, the falling away of the church must take place before the Rapture. If you hold to this view, then the falling away would be a sign that would precede the Rapture. It must be if you read it that way.

If the apostasy is the church falling away from the faith, then Paul is saying essentially that they will know when the Tribulation is about to start because of the worldwide rejection of Christ by the body of Christ. This is problematic because the Rapture by definition has no signs to precede it. It is a hidden, secret event, of which only the Father knows the timing: "But of that day and hour no one knows, not even the angels of heaven, nor the Son, but the Father alone" (Matt. 24:36).

In this incorrect scenario, not only will the Thessalonians (and therefore all believers) be witness to the church falling away, but they will also witness the "man of lawlessness" being revealed. Paul links these two things together in the verse in question. To put it another way, Paul is saying that they would know that they were in the Tribulation if the apostasy had happened AND the Antichrist was revealed. The latter obviously had not happened at the time of Paul's letter. They would have known (because Paul taught them) that the Tribulation begins with the Antichrist making the covenant with Israel (Dan. 9:27). This confirms that the Day of the Lord is analogous with the seventieth week of Daniel.

An even greater problem with the falling away from the faith scenario is the definition of the word *apostasy* (Greek—*apostasia*). It does not mean falling away from the faith. It simply means to depart from, separate from, move away from, or leave. It is a verb with no object noun (technically, it is a gerund, which is a verb that functions as a noun). In other words, faith, or belief in Jesus, is inappropriately inserted into the passage as an object to quantify or explain the falling away.

Apostasia is a derivative of the word *aphestemi*, which means to flee from, desert, or go away. Faith is nowhere to be found in the passage in 2 Thessalonians. It is assumed. Without the word *faith*, the passage is simply saying that the departure, or departing, must come first.

It is significant to note also that many of the early Bibles used *departing* in the passage for the translation of *apostasia*.

- Latin Vulgate (405)—*discessio* (Latin): withdrawal, dispersion
- Tyndale Bible (1525)—departing
- Coverdale Bible (1535)—departing
- Geneva Bible (1587)—departing

Finally, notwithstanding the definition of the word *apostasia*, Departure or Rapture makes perfect sense in the context. "Falling away from the faith" is incongruent. It does not make sense. Contextually, it is a piece of coal in a basket of apples.

The "falling away from the faith" translation comes out of nowhere, and there is no other passage in Scripture that indicates there will be a mass rejection of the faith by the church. Some point to Matthew 24:12, but you must really strain reason to get that out of the verse. Also, Matthew 24 is prophesying about conditions that will exist DURING the tribulation for the Jews, not prior to it.

Paul was attempting to calm the believers in Thessalonica. They were panicked that they were amid the Day of the Lord, or Tribulation. This is the context.

Paul starts the segment in chapter 2 verse 1 by setting the context "with regard to the coming of our lord Jesus Christ, and our gathering together to Him." This is the concern of the church. They thought they had missed the DEPARTURE! Paul is saying in chapter 2 verse 3 that the Day of the Lord (Tribulation) will not come unless the DEPARTURE comes first! There is no mass rejection of the faith by the church prophesied in the Bible.

6

Three Bankable Scriptural Truths That Guarantee the Church Will Be Raptured Prior to the Tribulation

1. *1 Thessalonians 1:10—"And to wait for His Son from heaven, whom He raised from the dead, that is Jesus, <u>who delivers us from the wrath to come</u>."*

Really, this verse is all you need to be confident that the church will be raptured prior to the Tribulation. The word *delivers* in this verse is *ruomai* in Greek, which means "to draw to oneself as if dragging or pulling to rescue from danger."

The word *from* in Greek is *ek*, which means "out of." A better translation of this passage would then actually be this: "Jesus, who will pull us up to Himself to rescue us out the way of the wrath that is coming."

This passage gives a much different picture than the picture put forth by those who advocate for a mid- or post-Tribulation Rapture. Their belief is that God will give the grace necessary to face all the horror and suffering that will take place during the seventieth week of Daniel.

I don't know about you, but that doesn't sound like being dragged out of the way of the wrath. And it certainly does not give me much comfort or peace of mind. It is no wonder why there is such a profitable business out there keeping the fear going by many preachers and authors in various media. Jim Bakker, for instance, is constantly hawking survival products on his show. End-times survival sells!

This verse indicates a much more drastic action than just being provided grace or strength. It is saying that Jesus is going to pull us up to Himself and out of the world before the wrath of God is poured out on creation during the Tribulation.

2. *Paul said that the Rapture will precede the Day of the Lord and the revealing of the Antichrist.*

> Now we request you, brethren, with regard to the coming of our Lord Jesus Christ, and our gathering together to Him, that you may not be quickly shaken from your composure or be disturbed either by a spirit or a message or a letter as if from us, to the effect that the day of the Lord has come. Let no one in any way deceive you, for IT WILL NOT COME UNLESS THE DEPARTURE COMES FIRST, and the man of lawlessness is revealed, the son of destruction. (2 Thess. 2:3)

I go into greater detail in my chapter "The Great Falling Away of the Church," but this verse is not saying the Day of the Lord will come after the "falling away from the faith," which is how most interpret it. Most translations say "apostasy" where I have "departure."

The Greek word *apostasia* means "departure" or "leaving." There is no quantifying noun. That is to say, neither of the words *faith* or *truth* is there. By itself, *apostasia* simply means "departure, leaving, or moving away from."

In this context, Paul is saying that the Rapture or Departure will come before the Day of the Lord. "Day of the Lord" is a Hebrew idiom for the seven-year period of judgment or Tribulation before the return of the King of Kings.

The Thessalonians thought they had been left behind and that the day of the Lord had come. Paul is clearly talking about the Rapture when he says, "With regard to the coming of our Lord...

and our gathering together to Him," and he uses the word *apostasia* as another way of describing it.

Paul says the order of events is this:

A. The Departure will happen, and then
B. the man of lawlessness will be revealed before the Day of the Lord.

The Antichrist will not be revealed until the church departs, which brings us to the third truth that guarantees the church will be raptured before the Tribulation begins.

3. *The restrainer is the Holy Spirit, and when He is removed, the Antichrist will be revealed.*

> For the mystery of lawlessness is already at work;
> only he who now restrains will do so until he is
> taken out of the way. (2 Thess. 2:7)

I go into much more detail about why the restrainer is the Holy Spirit in my articles "Michael the Restrainer?" and "Who or What Is the Restrainer?"

The Holy Spirit clearly is the restrainer. Paul is reiterating something he has undoubtedly gone over with the Thessalonians thoroughly in the past, namely that the Antichrist will not be revealed until the Holy Spirit removes Himself from the world.

Ergo, when the Holy Spirit is removed, the church is removed because the Holy Spirit resides in the body of Christ! This is what Paul says in 2 Thessalonians 2:3. The Departure comes first (Holy Spirit is removed), and then the Antichrist is revealed. Paul's comforting message is NOT that the church will be given grace to endure the Tribulation but that the church WILL NOT go through the Tribulation!

The Thessalonians were obviously disturbed and shaken by the thought that the Day of the Lord had come and that they were going to go through the Tribulation. If Paul had taught that the church would go through the Tribulation, then why wasn't Paul reminding them that God would give them strength and grace to endure the unprecedented sufferings, horrors, and tortures that will come during that time? Instead, he reminds them of the sequence of events leading up to the Tribulation. Ponder that for a minute! Christians are not supposed to prepare for the Tribulation!

The bottom line is that we, the body of Christ, should not be worried about the Tribulation—not because somehow we will be able to endure it by faith, but because we are not going to be here when the Antichrist is revealed and the Tribulation begins.

That really is the message in First and Second Thessalonians. Paul was trying to get them to quit worrying about it and focus on the real mission. Our mission is NOT to get ready to go through the Tribulation. It is to grow the kingdom of God by reaching the lost.

One last thought: Peter said that judgment begins now with the household of God.

> For it is time for judgment to begin with the household of God; and if it begins with us first, what will be the outcome for those who do not obey the gospel of God? (1 Peter 4:17)

As Christians, if we are trying to live by faith in this corrupt world, then we all will suffer—in varying degrees, but suffer nonetheless. This life is OUR tribulation and judgment, OUR trial and testing. We will not be here for the world's. Now that is real comfort!

7
The First Resurrection

> The rest of the dead did not come to life until the
> thousand years were completed. This is the first
> resurrection. (Rev. 20:5)

I watched a video that was sent to me by a friend who asked for
my thoughts about it. It was a teaching by a minister named David
Asscherick. His topic was the millennial kingdom—its description
and nature. He made quite a few incorrect assertions, but the one
I am going to focus on here is that there will be no living mortals
during the millennial period.

His basis for saying that there will be no living people is the
verse above, Revelation 20:5. He said all the righteous (throughout
history) will be resurrected at Jesus's return, and all the believers who
are alive at that time (who survive the Tribulation) will be translated
up to meet Jesus in the air. This is not true as I will demonstrate. He
also said all the wicked who are alive at His return will be slain. This
much is true (Rev. 19:15, 21).

What Asscherick did was declare that the resurrection in
Revelation 20:5 is the same resurrection as 1 Thessalonians 4:14.
This is something many Christians make the mistake of doing. He
based that on the fact that Revelation 20:5 says it is the first resurrection; therefore, it must be the same resurrection as 1 Thessalonians
4:14.

It follows, he asserts, that all the righteous will be glorified, and
all the wicked will be dead, and thus, there will be no mortal beings

during the one-thousand-year kingdom when Jesus reigns from Jerusalem.

To boil it down, Asscherick is saying that the Rapture happens at Jesus's return to earth (post-Tribulation Rapture). According to Asscherick, right before Jesus lands on the Mount of Olives, all the dead in Christ are raised, and those believers who are alive at that moment are translated or raptured and meet the Lord in the air (and then do an immediate U-turn to follow Christ to earth). The problem, however, is that Asscherick completely skipped over Revelation 20:4.

> And I saw thrones, and they sat upon them, and judgment was given to them. And I saw the souls of THOSE WHO HAD BEEN BEHEADED BECAUSE OF THE TESTIMONY OF JESUS and because of the Word of God, and THOSE WHO HAD NOT WORSHIPPED THE BEAST OR HIS IMAGE, AND HAD NOT RECEIVED THE MARK UPON THEIR FOREHEAD AND UPON THEIR HAND; and THEY CAME TO LIFE and reigned with Christ for a thousand years.

This verse makes perfectly clear that the first resurrection stated in verse 5 is the resurrection of the righteous who die during the Tribulation (Rev. 6:9; 13:12–17; 14:9–11). All he had to do was look at the cross references in the margin of his Bible. The context determines the meaning of "first resurrection."

The resurrection in Revelation 20:4–5 is not the first resurrection EVER; it is the first resurrection in the context of the second coming of Christ right before the beginning of the millennial kingdom. Clearly, this is not the first resurrection. The first resurrection was Jesus Christ! So the context must define the statement.

The second resurrection in this context is the resurrection of the unsaved dead (those whose names are not in the Book of Life) at the end of the millennial kingdom (Rev. 20:13).

Asscherick also completely overlooks Revelation 20:7–8 with his assertion that there are no living mortals during the millennial kingdom. These verses clearly point out that there will be nations all over the earth that Satan tempts and gathers for war when he is released at the end of the one thousand years. Asscherick's explanation for this is that these people are the wicked who are raised from the dead in Revelation 20:12–13.

The problem with that is that the second resurrection takes place AFTER Satan's brief uprising. The resurrection of the wicked who are slain at Jesus's coming are raised at the end of the millennial kingdom AFTER the Satan-led insurrection (Rev. 20:13) as are the wicked who revolt at the end of the one thousand years.

It never ceases to amaze how doctrines and teachings can come about by taking things out of their proper context or chronological order.

8

The Days of Noah

> For the coming of the Son of Man will be just
> like the days of Noah. (Matt. 24:37)

There are numerous ideas on what the phrase "days of Noah" means. I think everyone agrees that it is referring to the period that immediately precedes the return of Christ. The question becomes whether it is the period of time before the Rapture or Jesus's actual return to earth.

As always, I believe the context will reveal the correct meaning. So let us first start with understanding who Jesus is speaking to in this chapter and what the subject matter is. Follow along in Matthew 24. It is one of the most incredible, jam-packed end-times passages in all of Scripture.

Jesus is speaking to his Jewish disciples. Remember, Jesus said that His focus is the children of Israel. These people are whom Jesus made a priority to preach to and disciple: "But he answered and said, 'I was sent only to the lost sheep of the house of Israel'" (Matt. 15:24).

Jesus trained others to reach the rest of the world. His focus was Israel. It is critical that Christians resist inserting the church into passages where it does not belong. Matthew 24 is one of those passages.

The subject matter is the seventieth week of Daniel, otherwise known as the seven years of Tribulation. This period occurs after the Rapture. I will not go into a pre-Tribulation Rapture defense in this article. Scripture is crystal clear that the church will be evacuated prior to the beginning of the Tribulation. Read the previous chapters

"Michael the Restrainer?" and "Who or What Is the Restrainer?" The restrainer is key to understanding the Rapture.

In Matthew 24:3, the disciples ask Jesus to tell them when the temple will be destroyed and what will be the sign of His coming and end of the age. There are two questions. Matthew only records Jesus's answer to the second question. Luke records answers to both questions in Luke 21.

In verse 4, Jesus begins describing the signs that will lead to His return to earth on Mount Zion. Verses 4–8 are the description of the birth pangs described in Revelation 6–8, otherwise known as the seven seals.

It is important to realize that Jesus is prophesying in this context. He is speaking past the immediate audience to a future generation of Jewish believers in the Tribulation. Why do I say that? Because his disciples will not be on the earth during the seven-year Tribulation period. This prophecy is for a generation that turns to the Lord during the seventieth week of Daniel.

In verse 13, Jesus tells this future generation that if they survive the seven years, they will be saved or rescued. They will go on to live forever beginning with the one-thousand-year millennial kingdom. This verse has nothing to do with the salvation of their soul (see the chapter "The One Who Endures to the End.")

Continuing in verse 15, Jesus tells this future generation that when they see the abomination of desolation standing in the holy place (just as Daniel spoke of), they are to drop everything and flee Jerusalem immediately. The abomination of desolation is the Antichrist standing in the holy of holies in the temple that is yet to be rebuilt (Dan. 9:27, 2 Thess. 2:3–4). This will occur in the middle of the seven-year Tribulation.

Jesus tells this future generation that they are not to come out of hiding in the wilderness if they hear that Jesus has come to earth (vss. 23–26). He tells them that there will be no doubt when He comes because they will see the Shekinah Glory in the sky when Jesus comes on the clouds (vss. 27–30)!

Upon His return and the destruction of the armies of Satan (Rev. 19), He will gather all the righteous Jews on earth and bring them to the promised land to dwell during the millennial kingdom (vs. 31).

He then promises that the generation of Jews that sees all these events take place, from the opening of the seals to His coming in the clouds, will not be completely destroyed before everything concludes, including Jesus's return. That is what He is saying in verse 34.

> Now learn the parable from the fig tree: when its branch has already become tender, and puts forth its leaves, you know that summer is near; even so you to, when you see all these things, recognize that He is near, right at the door. Truly I say to you, this generation will not pass away until all these things take place. (Matt. 24:32–34)

Jesus's reference to the parable of the fig tree pertains to the Messiah returning to earth and ruling from Jerusalem. It is another Jewish idiom; it is not for the church. In other words, it is not about Jesus's coming for the church; it is about Jesus coming to rule from Zion and fulfilling all the prophecies regarding the Messiah and Israel going back to Abraham.

Jesus is saying that when the believing Jews see all the signs of His return to earth—from the seal judgments to the gospel of the kingdom preached to every corner of earth, from the abomination of desolation to the false reports of Messiah when they are in the wilderness—they are to know and believe that they will <u>NOT</u> pass away before He sets foot on Mount Zion. That is the importance of the phrase, "Truly I say to you." He is saying that a remnant will survive. You must stay in context!

This is what Jesus is emphasizing in Matthew 24:22: "And unless those days had been cut short, no life would have been saved; but for the sake of the elect those days shall be cut short." This is the context! We will talk about the elect in chapter 10.

Then in verse 36, Jesus pivots and now speaks directly to His present company. The next part of the chapter is specifically directed at the disciples. Consequently, this part of the message is also for the church. Why? Because it is information relevant to all believers prior to the tribulation (Mark 13:37).

> But of the day and hour, no one knows, not even the angels of heaven, nor the Son, but the Father alone. (24:36)

What day and hour? Here, the context is Jesus referring to the Day of the Lord (1 Thess. 5:2, 2 Thess. 2:2, 2 Peter 3:10). The expression "Day of the Lord" is an idiom or theme that references the period of the judgment of the world and the return of the Messiah to earth. It is characterized as coming like a thief in the night. The Rapture is that singular event that there is NO sign for and that cannot be predicted.

The mistake that many in the church make is trying to categorize all the end-time events in Matthew 24:6–8 as signs leading up to the Rapture. They are not. They are signs that verify the Tribulation is in full swing. They are signs for the elect who come out of the Tribulation.

So Jesus tells them that the coming of the Son of Man will be just like the days of Noah. What Jesus is referring to here in verse 37 is the circumstances that will immediately precede and follow the Rapture.

What He tells His disciples (and in turn, us) is that life will be very mundane compared to the Tribulation. In the days of Noah, people were living their lives as if there were no judgment coming, all the while as Noah was building the ark over a period of 120 years. When Noah went into the ark, Jesus said they did not understand. In other words, they undoubtedly looked upon Noah as a fool. It was not until the floodwaters were raging that they realized what was going on. So it will be when the church is rescued and disappears.

In Matthew 24:40–41, Jesus describes that day and hour of the rapture: "Two men in the field and one will be taken, two women at the mill and one will be taken."

They—the unsaved earth dwellers—will be perplexed for a time. They will not understand what happened to all the people who were raptured. Eventually, they may even forget about the disappearance of a billion people from the earth; that is, until the seals are opened (1 Thess. 5:3, 2 Thess. 2:8–12). Then they will realize that destruction is upon them, and it will be too late.

Those who will be dwelling on earth when the Antichrist comes to power and establishes order will be content and will go about their business as if nothing is happening. They will be eating and drinking and giving in marriage because they believe that all is well. Paul says in 1 Thessalonians 5:3 that they will be exclaiming, "Peace and safety!"

The point that Jesus is making is that the "days of Noah" is a reference to people being unbelieving, hard-hearted, and surprised when the Day of the Lord finally does come. It is not about end-time events leading up to His return. It is about people not believing that Jesus is coming.

What Jesus tells his disciples is precisely what Paul told the Thessalonians.

> Therefore, be on the alert, for you do not know which day your Lord is coming. (Matt. 24:42)

> But you brethren, are not in darkness, that the day should overtake you like a thief; for you are all sons of light and sons of day. We are not of night nor of darkness; so then let us not sleep as others do, but let us be alert and sober. (1 Thess. 5:4–6)

We ought not be taken by surprise.

9
Birth Pangs

> But all these things are merely the beginning of
> birth pangs. (Matt. 24:8)

There is a lot of talk about the birth pangs these days. Many Christians are saying that we are seeing them now—earthquakes, wars and rumors of wars, pestilence, and even the potential for famines. Are we really experiencing the events that Jesus, Paul, and John prophesied? No, we are not.

We are not seeing the birth pangs that were prophesied because they are Tribulation events. We are not in the Tribulation. Are these types of things occurring today? Absolutely, but nowhere near the level of magnitude as will happen in the seven-year Tribulation period before the return of Christ to earth.

It's easy to take the passage in Matthew where Jesus is describing wars, famine, earthquakes, lawlessness, and love growing cold out of context. These things have been occurring since the flood. But that does not mean they are the specific things foretold as the birth pangs.

In Matthew 24, Jesus is clearly speaking about the Tribulation. His outline of things to come in response to the disciples' question—"What will be the sign of Your coming and the end of the age?"—fits in precisely with the format we find in Daniel 9, 1 Thessalonians 4 and 5, and Revelation. The format, or timeline, is as follows:

1. The church is evacuated to heaven (1 Thess. 1:10; 1 Thess. 4:15; 2 Thess. 2:1–3)

2. The Antichrist is revealed (2 Thess. 2:3–12)
3. Peace and safety on earth (1 Thess. 5:3; 2 Thess. 2:8–11)
4. An agreement is made between Israel and Antichrist, probably to allow Israel to build the temple and sacrifice in peace (Dan. 9:27)
5. The birth pangs begin (Matt. 24:6; Mark 13:7–13; 1 Thess. 4:15–5:3; Rev. 6)
6. The two witnesses are killed (Rev. 11:7)
7. Antichrist stops the sacrifices and enters the holy of holies in the new temple in the middle of the Tribulation, declaring himself to be God and Savior (Dan. 9:27; Matt. 24:15; Mark 13:14; 2 Thess. 2:4)
8. Jews flee Jerusalem and elsewhere into the wilderness for three and a half years (Hosea 2:14–16; Matt. 24:16–20; Mark 13:14–18; Rev. 12:6)
9. Satan is thrown down from heaven and permanently shut out of the throne room of God (Rev. 12:9–10)
10. Satan tries to destroy the Jews in the wilderness and the rest of the Jews on earth (Rev. 12:13–17)
11. Armageddon takes place (Ezek. 38–39:8; Zech. 14:2–3; Rev. 19:11–21)
12. Jesus returns to earth at the end of the seven years (Zech. 14:4; Matt. 24:30; Rev. 19:11)

So we see there are four other major events that will take place before the birth pangs begin. None of these events have happened. One of the main reasons we put the beginning of birth pangs at the number 5 position is because Jesus is answering the question from His disciples: "What will be the sign of Your coming, and of the end of the age?"

The birth pangs occur at the end of the age. They do not occur throughout the age or ages. And they are signs that verify that the Day of the Lord has come. The Day of the Lord is an idiom that essentially means the judgment of the world up to and including the return of Christ to earth, i.e., the Tribulation.

This is what Paul explains in First Thessalonians. In his condensed summary of the Tribulation, Paul says the birth pangs begin after the Rapture and then sometime after peace and safety have been established on earth by Antichrist (1 Thess. 5:2–3).

The birth pangs that Jesus lay out in Matthew 24 match up with the seal judgments in Revelation 6.

	Revelations 6	Matthew 24
False Messiahs/Prophets	6:2	24:5, 11
Wars and Rumors of Wars	6:2-4	24:6-7
International Discord	6:3-4	24:7
Famine	6:5-8	24:7
Pestilence	6:8	
Persecution/Martyrdom	6:9-11	24:9
Earthquakes	6:12	24:7
Cosmic Phenomena	6:12-14	

It is also important to remember that Jesus said that the trials he listed are just the beginning of birth pangs. The pangs continue throughout the seven years all the way until the firmament is ripped open and Christ is seen coming to earth in the clouds. They include the trumpet judgments and the bowl judgments of Revelation.

The birth pangs are the judgment of the world. As birth pangs do, these judgments get longer and more painful up until the birth, which is Jesus's return and reclamation of earth.

We are not seeing the birth pangs. But with the earthquakes, the locust plagues in Africa and the Middle East, the coronavirus travesty, and now rampant lawlessness, perhaps the Lord is giving a little warning of what is about to come upon the whole earth when the restrainer is removed.

10
Who Are the Elect?

> And unless those days had been cut short, no life
> would have been saved; but for the sake of the
> elect those days shall be cut short. (Matt. 24:22)

> For false Christs and false prophets will arise and
> will show great signs and wonders, so as to mis-
> lead, if possible, even the elect. (Matt. 24:24)

> And He will send forth His angels with a great
> trumpet and they will gather together His elect
> from the four winds, from one end of the sky to
> the other. (Matt. 24:31)

The answer to the question "Who are the elect?" is, it depends on
the context.

A client and friend of mine asked me to listen to a preacher by
the name of Irvin Baxter. She listens to him regularly and asked me
to give her my thoughts about his doctrinal positions. The video I
watched told me everything I needed to know about how he inter-
prets Scripture regarding the church and the Departure (or Rapture).

Baxter said that the church will go through the seventieth week
of Daniel, aka the Tribulation. He argues that the church is raptured
at the end of the Tribulation (post-Tribulation). He says the basis for
this belief are the three verses mentioned above and that the elect in
these passages is the church. Therefore, according to Baxter, the gathering of the elect in verse 31 is the Rapture of the church.

Baxter says Matthew 24:24 is a warning to the church not to be deceived by false rumors of Christ's return. They would know He was returning because they, the church, would see him coming in the sky.

Baxter said that the elect in Matthew and the other Gospels was the same elect as in Romans 8:33. He said Paul was using the word with reference to members of the body of Christ, the church; therefore, Matthew was also referring to the church.

Baxter's explanation is another example of inserting the church into passages where it does not belong. The context dictates who the elect is. In Matthew, the elect are the believing Jews in Jerusalem during the Tribulation. In Romans, the elect are believers who are the body of Christ, the church. It is that simple.

The word *elect* simply means "chosen ones." There is no basis to conclude that the chosen ones referred to by Paul are the same chosen ones in Matthew, Mark, and Luke. The context in Matthew, Mark, and Luke are the same. It is about the Jews who have fled Jerusalem into the wilderness after the Antichrist defiles the holy of holies in the coming third temple.

It is the Jews who are told not to come out of hiding in the wilderness when they hear the rumors that the Messiah is around, not the church. That is the elect in the context whom Jesus will save in verse 22. They—the believing Jews—are the ones whom Satan will be trying to destroy by a flood in Revelation 12. The context in Revelation 12 is the same as in Matthew 24:15–31.

Isaiah 11:11–12 says the Jews will be regathered a second time. This passage in Isaiah prophesies that it is the DISPERSED OF JUDAH who will be regathered from the four corners of the earth. Isaiah and Matthew are talking about the children of Abraham, Isaac, and Jacob, who will be gathered, NOT THE CHURCH!

The first regathering of the Jews has happened. The second regathering is what is prophesied in Matthew 24 and Isaiah 11. These passages are not talking about the Rapture. They are describing a gathering of all the Jews on earth into the promised land for the millennial kingdom.

The elect in the Gospels are not the church; they are Jews who have believed in Christ the Messiah during the Tribulation. The gathering in Matthew is the gathering of all the believing Jews to the promised land when Christ returns to earth. The Rapture or Departure of the church takes place prior to the Tribulation.

11

Are Travel and Technology a Last-Days Bible Prophecy?

> But as for you, Daniel, conceal these words and
> seal up the book until the end of time; many will
> go back and forth, and knowledge will increase.
> (Dan. 12:4)

You hear about this one all the time. In the last days, people will be traveling all over the world because of jet airliners. Also, because of technology (meaning Internet), knowledge is going to increase exponentially. This is how many in the evangelical mainstream interpret this passage.

In other words, going back and forth means increased travel capabilities, and knowledge increasing refers to having instant access to information. This is a perfect example of putting something into a passage that has no business being there. The verse is saying no such things.

The last four chapters of Daniel are visions pertaining to Daniel's people (Dan. 9:24). Who are Daniel's people? They are the Jewish people. Daniel was Jewish, taken into captivity by the Babylonians.

In Daniel 9, Daniel discovers in the book of Isaiah Israel's judgment prophecy that resulted in the captivity in Babylon. Then Daniel makes a deep and impassioned prayer for God's mercy on Israel. As a result of Daniel's supplication, Gabriel comes to Daniel and lays out the future of Israel with respect to the coming kingdoms of Persia, Greece, and Rome. These visions span chapters 9–11. After revealing these visions, Daniel is told to conceal the words and seal them up until the end of time.

So how does one extrapolate airplanes and technology (Internet) from this verse? One does this by going off the rails and making wild speculations rather than staying in context. Chapter 12 verse 4 has the answer right in it.

Going back and forth simply means searching the Scriptures and other reference material for understanding of the visions that Daniel was told to conceal. In fact, some may even stumble on this book as a resource after the Rapture to understand what is happening.

And the knowledge that will increase is that understanding of the prophecy. It is all about Daniel's people, the Jews, coming to an understanding of the Messiah and all the events that are occurring during the seventieth week of Daniel, or the Tribulation period.

The previous verse explains this very thing. In chapter 12 verse 3, it says that many of Daniel's people (Jews) will lead other Jews to righteousness. Leading to righteousness means leading them to the true Messiah and salvation. They will lead other Jews to righteousness because they have searched the Scriptures, gained understanding, and shared this knowledge with many other Jews. Therefore, knowledge will increase (see also Amos 8:12).

This will happen during the last part of the vision in Daniel of the Roman Empire, the empire that will be revived under the Antichrist. Daniel 12 is specifically and exclusively a prophecy about the seventieth week of Daniel, otherwise known as the seven-year Tribulation.

Daniel 12:4 is not about planes, trains, and the Internet. It is about seeking, finding, and proclaiming the knowledge of the truth.

12
The Greatest Sign

> Then it will happen on that day that the Lord will
> again recover the second time with His hand the
> remnant of His people, who will remain, from
> Assyria, Egypt, Pathros, Cush, Elam, Shinar,
> Hamath and from the coastlands of the sea. 12.
> And He will lift up a standard for the nations,
> and will assemble the banished ones of Israel, and
> will gather the dispersed of Judah from the four
> corners of the earth. (Isaiah 11:10–11)

(This was originally published in August 2017.) We are living in a time unique to every past generation. Of course, every past generation could say that. But there is something in our time that does not compare to anything in the past.

Isaiah prophesied about a coming event that will take place when Jesus returns to earth to establish the kingdom of God with Jerusalem as the capital. At that time, one of the things that will happen is that all the surviving believing Jews will be gathered from all over earth and brought back to Israel where they will live in the territory promised to Abraham. Jesus declared this will be a supernatural gathering in Matthew 24:30–31, saying that when He returns, He will send His angels to bring them. The interesting thing about the passage in Isaiah 11 is that it is referring to a second regathering from all over the world. What about the first?

This year, November 29, 2017, marks the seventieth anniversary of the UN resolution that allowed for the establishment of a

Jewish state. A government was formed, and six months later, the United States became the first country to formally recognize Israel. Harry Truman famously declared, "I am Cyrus," hearkening back to the ancient king of Persia.

After conquering the Babylonian empire, Cyrus allowed the captive Jews to return to Judah and rebuild Jerusalem and the temple that Nebuchadnezzar destroyed. Many Jews were taken into captivity by the Babylonians, and they remained so for seventy years until Cyrus. This was a fulfillment of Isaiah 44:28.

Some think that the first regathering took place when the Jews from the Babylonian captivity returned to Judah. This does not make sense because there were still plenty of Jews that remained after Nebuchadnezzar conquered it. Not all the inhabitants were taken into captivity.

Nebuchadnezzar actually left a government in place with Zedekiah as king, albeit a puppet. Reasonable calculations based on historical records, including Jeremiah, estimate that only one eighth to one fourth of the inhabitants of Judah were taken into exile.

In AD 70, Judah ceased to exist when the Romans wiped out Jerusalem, destroyed the temple, and drove all the Jews from their homes, scattering them throughout Europe, Africa, and Asia. This is known as the Diaspora. The northern kingdom of Israel had already vanished into exile in 722 BC after being conquered by the Assyrians.

Aliyah

The beautiful land became desolate and empty of Abraham's descendants for almost two thousand years. In the late 1800s, the Zionist movement began, and along with it, aliyah. Aliyah means "to go up," as into Jerusalem, and it came to signify the mass migration of Jews back to the land of Israel. From 1881 to 1939, in a series of waves of aliyah, close to five hundred thousand Jews moved to Israel, mostly from Eastern Europe and Russia.

Since Israel became a recognized nation again in 1948, Jews from all over the world have poured in. It was reported in 2003 that for the first time in almost two thousand years, Israel held the highest concentration of Jews in the world, surpassing the United States. Today, there are nearly seven million Jews in Israel, and migration has essentially gone to zero. It appears that Yahweh may be close to finished with the first regathering.

Scripture is clear that the Jewish nation had to exist again before the return of Christ. Jesus left a message for future Jewish believers in the Tribulation that when they see the Antichrist standing in the holy of holies in the coming rebuilt temple, they are to flee Jerusalem (Matt. 24:15).

Even though there is no sign required before the Rapture takes place, the regathering of the Jewish people back into the promised land is the single greatest biblical sign that we are living in the last days. It is a partial fulfillment of Isaiah 11:11. Maranatha!

Part 1 Summary

I hope the puzzle pieces are coming together for you. In this first part, I have demonstrated that the Rapture must come before the Tribulation. Two essential and absolute reasons are that the restrainer is the Holy Spirit and is keeping the Antichrist, or lawless one, from being revealed. The Antichrist is revealed prior to the Tribulation. Therefore, the church must be removed prior to the Tribulation because the Holy Spirit is in the church. That is what Paul teaches in Second Thessalonians.

He also told the Thessalonians that the Rapture, or Departure, must come before the Day of the Lord, or judgment. The Departure and the restrainer are inextricably connected.

PART 2

The body of Christ is not supposed to be concerned about the Tribulation. True believers will not be going through it. But it is important to understand what the Bible says about it.

The Word of God teaches that there is a beginning, middle, and end to the seven-year tribulation, otherwise known as the seventieth week of Daniel.

At the beginning of the Tribulation, the Antichrist is going to enter into a major agreement or contract with the nation of Israel. The passage in Daniel 9:27 refers to Israel as "the many." It is a term used numerous times for Daniel's people, or the Jews. It says the Antichrist will make a "firm covenant," or strong pledge, for one week, which is seven years.

In the middle of the seven years, Daniel says that the Antichrist will put a stop to sacrifices. In Matthew 24:15, Jesus says that the Antichrist will enter the holy of holies of a rebuilt temple. This is the most holy part of the temple where only the high priest could enter and where God dwelt as the Holy Spirit. In 2 Thessalonians 2:4, Paul reiterates what Jesus says. He says the "man of lawlessness" (another reference to the Antichrist) will take his seat in the temple and declare himself to be the Most High God.

Because the Antichrist does not stop the sacrifices and commit "the abomination of desolation" until the halfway point of the Tribulation, this leads me to believe that the agreement in Daniel 9 has something to do with allowing the Jews to rebuild the temple and also begin sacrificing.

A couple of other significant things happen in the middle of the Tribulation. Prior to the Antichrist entering the holy of holies in the new temple, the two witnesses of Revelation 11, who have been preaching and prophesying for the first three and a half years, are killed.

The world is going to be firmly in the grasp of Antichrist at this time. The earth will be a horribly wicked place, so much so that the entire world will be watching as the two witnesses are killed and their lifeless bodies lay in the street in Jerusalem. The people of earth will celebrate and give gifts to each other as if it is Christmas (Rev. 11:3–10).

Until television and the Internet came along, it was difficult to understand how the entire world could watch this evil spectacle in real time.

Jesus warned the Jews in Matthew 24 that when they see the Antichrist desecrate the temple and declare himself to be God, they are to flee immediately out of the city. Revelation 12 says the fleeing Jews will hide in the wilderness, and there they will be supernaturally cared for by God as He did the Israelites in the wilderness after leaving Egypt.

When the Antichrist declares himself to be God, Satan is cast out of the throne room of heaven forever and thrown down to earth (Rev. 12:9). When this happens, Scripture says Satan realizes that he does not have much time, and so he multiplies his efforts to wipe out the Jews.

The spiritual battle being waged is a battle for the kingdom on earth. Satan has been bound and determined to destroy all the Jews since Christ came. It is his goal to make God out as a liar by destroying the Jews. God promised all the land that was shown to Abraham in Genesis 15:18. That promise has yet to be fulfilled completely.

If there are no Jews living on the earth when Christ returns, then Satan will have subverted the promise to Abraham and his descendants. This is why Jesus was so serious when He said this in Matthew 24:22: "And unless those days had been cut short, no life would have been saved; but for the sake of the elect, those days shall be cut short." I go into this in detail in chapter 18.

But we know the ending. Jesus will return and save the elect Jews, and they will recognize Him as the Messiah, crying out, "Blessed is He who comes in the name of the Lord" (Matt. 23:39)!

The battle of Armageddon will be raging when He returns with the church, and He will destroy all the wicked with the breath of His mouth.

All the believing Jews who survive the Tribulation will be brought into the promised land from all over the world. Jesus Christ will reign from Jerusalem for the next one thousand years.

The following are several articles that address various aspects of the seventieth week of Daniel leading up to the physical return of Christ. In that vein, let us begin this second part with the very day that Jesus will return to earth.

13
Jubilee

> You shall thus consecrate the fiftieth year and proclaim a release through the land to all its inhabitants. It shall be a jubilee for you, and each of you shall return to his own property, and each of you shall return to his family. (Lev. 25:10)

I am going to make the case that Jesus will return to earth, setting foot in Jerusalem, on the Feast of Atonement in the Year of Jubilee, fulfilling the representation of that particular feast as well as the Year of Jubilee.

I will also make the case that if the Year of Jubilee is a date that is still kept in heaven (which I believe is), then the next fiftieth year will be either 2027 or 2028. It follows that if that is the date that Jesus returns to earth, it would be at the end of the seven-year Tribulation.

That being the case, the Rapture would be super-imminent if this next Jubilee is when Christ returns. The Rapture would be imminent because it takes place prior to the Tribulation.

No, I am not setting a date for the Rapture. Nor am I saying conclusively that Jesus will return to earth in 2027 or 2028. Even if I were saying that, it does not mean I am setting a date for the Rapture. That can happen any time before the Tribulation.

I do believe that Jesus will return on Jubilee. It just may not be the next Jubilee year. But honestly, I cannot see things continuing like this on earth for another fifty-seven years. The stage is rapidly being set for Antichrist.

The Year of Jubilee was a celebration required as part of the Mosaic Law in Leviticus 25. It mandates that all land be given back to the original owners at the end of seven Sabbaths of years, or forty-nine years. The fiftieth year was the Jubilee, which means "rams horn" in Hebrew.

It occurred on the tenth day of Tishri, which is the seventh month on the Hebrew calendar. That day was also the Day of Atonement, or Feast of Atonement, celebrated every year. It is one of the three fall feasts that were appointed by God to be celebrated by the Jews. Not only would land be returned but debts and indentured service will go away also.

It was the great reset, if you will. Its impact resulted in maintaining wealth distribution and prosperity for all. It kept the few from winding up with most of the nation's wealth. Frankly, it is something we need desperately in this current economy and world situation. But it also foreshadowed something else. Leviticus 25:23 is key to understanding this law.

> The land, moreover, shall not be sold permanently, <u>for the land is mine</u>; for you are but aliens and sojourners with me.

Ultimately, the Year of Jubilee represents the earth and everything in it going back to the original owner—God the Father through His Son Jesus Christ.

I believe the return of Jesus will be the fulfillment of the Feast of Atonement in the Year of Jubilee. The world will have gone through its cleansing, or atonement. This also brings into focus the other two fall feasts, the Feast of Trumpets and Feast of Tabernacles.

I have been kind of groping for years to understand how the fall feasts will be fulfilled. The spring feasts were all fulfilled when Jesus first came—Feast of Unleavened Bread, Passover, Feast of Firstfruits, and Pentecost.

Jesus fulfilled them with His life and death on the exact dates of the feasts at the time. I will not go into an explanation here on the spring feasts. You can research them easily. God lays all the feasts out in chapter 23 of Leviticus.

As we dive into it, I think it's critically important to understand that the feasts were God's appointed times for Israel. They were not meant for the church or anyone else to keep. That is what Leviticus 23:2 is clear about. God spoke to Moses, saying, "Speak to the sons of Israel, and say to them, 'The Lord's appointed times which you shall proclaim as holy convocations—My appointed times are these.'"

The Feast of Tabernacles follows Atonement on the fifteenth day of the same month. It represents God's desire and intention to dwell with man. It also symbolizes man's temporary condition and living on earth, which is why God told Israel that they were sojourners. This feast will literally be fulfilled right after Jesus returns when He sets up His dwelling in Jerusalem.

The one feast I am still not 100 percent sure about when and how it is fulfilled is Trumpets, which occurs on the first day of the seventh month.

The Feast of Trumpets is represented by the blowing of trumpets, or shofars (ram's horns). On that day, these horns will blow, declaring a time to rest (Lev. 23:24). That is all the Scripture says about it. We can see that it was the opening day of the month of Tishri and leading to the other feasts. I think of it like the trumpet at the Kentucky Derby signaling that the race is about to begin.

The question is, how will this be fulfilled? For now, I believe that it represents the heralding of Jesus's appearance in the Shekinah Glory when He returns to earth in Matthew 24:30–31.

> And then the sign of the Son of Man will appear in the sky, and then all the tribes of the earth will mourn, and they will see the Son of Man coming on the clouds of the sky with power and great glory.
> And He will send forth His angels WITH A GREAT TRUMPET and they will gather together His elect from the four winds, from one end of the sky to the other.

Remember, these feasts are for the Jews, and this message in Matthew is specifically for the Jews who will flee Jerusalem into the

Judean wilderness through the Valley of Achor to hide for the last three and a half years of the Tribulation.

In Matthew 24:24–26, Jesus is telling the Jews in the future, when they are hiding, to not come out of the hills based on rumors that Christ had returned. He tells them they will know when He comes because they will see Him coming in the sky with the shofars of heaven heralding His appearance.

The trumpets will signal that the waiting is over and that the time of rest has come for the elect, who are the Jews that Jesus is coming to rescue as promised in Matthew and prophesied in Revelation 12. The trumpet will signal to the elect and the angels. It does not necessarily mean that the angels gather the elect at that moment. The verse simply says that the Lord sends forth the angels. More about this later in the article.

So there is a sequence of events: Feast of Trumpets signals to prepare for the return of Jesus, Feast of Atonement and Year of Jubilee when Jesus returns to earth, and Feast of Tabernacles when Jesus dwells with man.

Now about 2027. I believe that Jesus was born in either 2 or 3 BC. I know many put it at 4 BC because of a belief that Herod died in 4 BC. I personally believe that Herod probably died in 1 BC. You can read a good article defending the 1 BC date at this link: https://www.ncregister.com/blog/jimmy-akin/ the-100-year-old-mistake-about-the-birth-of-jesus.

Luke's gospel gives credence to a 2 or 3 BC birth based on John the Baptist beginning his ministry in the fifteenth year of Tiberius (Luke 3:1). According to Luke, Jesus was about thirty years old. I take that to mean Jesus was in His thirtieth year but not yet to his thirtieth birthday.

This would make sense because Jesus began His ministry before his birthday, which was during the Feast of Booths. That would make Him a few days shy of His birthday when He announced His ministry on Atonement.

The fifteenth year of Tiberius Caesar equates to AD 29. Remember, the fifteenth year is the time between the completion of the fourteenth year and the completion of the fifteenth year, the same way a child's first year is the time between his birth and his first birthday.

Jesus's ministry starts somewhat after John's, but it does not appear to be exceedingly long after. Perhaps only a few weeks or months. That being the case, Jesus's ministry would begin at twenty-nine. If you count back thirty years, you will get to 2 BC or 3 BC (you must count year 0), depending on whether Tiberius's tenure was calculated from his crowning or from January 1.

When Jesus began His ministry, He did so on the Day of Atonement in the Year of Jubilee. We know this because when He announced it in the synagogue, He quoted Isaiah 61:1–2. The passage is a reference to the Year of Jubilee, or as Isaiah put it, the "favorable year of the Lord." Then Jesus said that "this Scripture has been fulfilled in [their] hearing."

Of course, Jesus left off "and the day of vengeance of our God" from the Isaiah text, which will be the part fulfilled when Jesus returns to earth at Armageddon.

Now, getting back to the next Year of Jubilee. It will either be the fall of 2027 or 2028, depending on the birth of Jesus in 3 or 2 BC. If it is 3 BC, then 2027. I lean toward 2 BC, which would make it 2028.

But the Rapture could happen anytime. We know there is going to be a period when the Antichrist establishes order in the world and then peace and prosperity (see the chapter "Times and Epochs"). It will be a golden era unlike anything the world has ever seen.

This golden age could last many months. The Antichrist will consolidate his power during this time. Then he will ignite the Tribulation when he completes the covenant or treaty with the nation of Israel (Dan. 9:27).

When that happens, which will be during the month of Tishri as well, then the seventieth week of Daniel will begin, otherwise known as the Tribulation. In fact, it is likely to be on Feast of Tabernacles, the fifteenth day of Tishri.

This date fits perfectly with my belief that the Antichrist will commit the abomination of desolation on Passover, the fifteenth day of the Hebrew month Nisan, which would be the exact midpoint of the seven-year Tribulation from Tishri 15.

The one potential problem I see with the scenario that I have outlined is the day of the fulfillment of the Feast of Trumpets. If it is literally fulfilled on the exact day, then that means that the heralding of the shofars would begin on Tishri 1, ten days before the appearance and coming of Christ to earth.

That is very possible. It is possible that the believing Jews, particularly those who are hiding in the wilderness, will hear the shofar blasts on Tishri 1 because God wishes to signal them and because the Jews are will be looking for that sign on that day. The Feast of Trumpets is a signal that the Jews are to prepare for the Feast of Atonement. Then ten days after the shofar blasts, the firmament rips open and Jesus descends.

It does not fit Matthew 24's order of things precisely if you interpret them in rigid chronological order. But it is possible that the trumpet and gathering in chapter 24 verse 31 stands by itself rather than being a continuation of verse 30.

Another option is that the fulfillment of the Feast of Trumpets does not happen on the specific day of Tishri 1, but it does happen in its proper sequence. The question then becomes, why would all the spring feasts be fulfilled precisely and one of the fall feasts not? That is a dilemma.

I lean to the idea that there will be trumpet blasts on Tishri 1 and that the elect in the wilderness will hear them, and they will "recognize that He is near, right at the door" even if it is not expressly found in Matthew or elsewhere. Feast of Trumpets will be fulfilled.

Israel does not currently celebrate the Year of Jubilee, and they have not since the northern tribes were conquered by the Assyrians in 722. But I believe God keeps the dates on His calendar and will through the millennial Kingdom (Ezekiel 46:17).

Jesus will return to earth in the Year of Jubilee on the Day of Atonement and reclaim the earth. Many believe that the book referred to in Revelation 5 is the ledger of all of God's possessions on earth—the title to all the land as well as everything else He is going to redeem. It makes sense to me. Everything belongs to Him. He is coming to get it all back. And it seems sooner rather than later.

14
The Valley of Achor

Therefore, behold, I will allure her, bring her into the wilderness, and speak kindly to her. Then I will give her her vineyards from there, and the Valley of Achor as a door of hope. And she will sing there as in the days of her youth, as in the day when she came up from the land of Egypt. And it will come about in that day, declares the Lord, that you will call Me "my husband" and will no longer call me "my master." (Hosea 2:14–16)

This is a gem of last-days prophecy tucked in the book of Hosea. It is a prophecy of hope to the nation of Israel and the sons and daughters of Abraham. It goes hand in hand with Matthew 24:15–18 and Revelation 12. It is a promise to the remnant that will survive the Tribulation, or seventieth week of Daniel.

Hosea was a contemporary of Isaiah and prophet to Israel. While Hosea is primarily a book of prophecy to Israel (as opposed to Judah when the kingdom was divided), I believe that the passage in question is really meant for all the descendants of Abraham. I will explain later in this article.

When the Antichrist takes his seat in the holy place as described in Matthew 24:15 and 2 Thessalonians 2:4, the Jews who believe in Jesus as Messiah at that time are warned to flee Jerusalem into the Judean wilderness.

The Valley of Achor is that doorway or passage of escape. If you go on Google Earth, you can see the valley heading east out of

Jerusalem. You can zoom in and get a particularly good picture of the valley. It lies in the center of the wilderness between Jerusalem and Jericho, just north of the Dead Sea.

Revelation 12:6 and 12:14 describe the scenario of Matthew 24:15–18. The "woman" (Israel) will flee into the wilderness and be "nourished" or taken care of for the last half of the seven-year Tribulation. The woman in Revelation 12 and "her" in Hosea 2 are both Israel.

The righteous Jews, who are in Israel and Jerusalem at the time of the abomination of desolation, will know about this way of escape (see the chapter "Are Travel and Technology a Last-Days Bible Prophecy?") and will be prepared.

When the time comes, dozens, hundreds, or maybe thousands of Jews will pour out of Jerusalem into the Valley of Achor and to a place of hiding in the wilderness where God will supernaturally care for Israel just as He did when Israel came out of Egypt.

Zechariah 14:5 also describes this same scenario: "And you will flee by the valley of My mountains, for the valley of the mountains will reach to Azel; yes, you will flee just as you fled before the earthquake in the days of Uzziah king of Judah. Then the Lord, my God, will come, and all the holy ones with Him!"

This passage is saying the same thing as Hosea and Revelation 12. The Jews will escape through the valley into the wilderness, and after three and a half years, the Lord will come with all the saints, and He will set foot on the Mount of Olives to save the elect (Zech. 14:4).

Not only is the text consistent with the those in Hosea, Matthew, and Revelation but also the strongest evidence suggests that Azel was very near to the Mount of Olives, only half a mile southeast, which is on the east side of Jerusalem. This would put it directly on the path of the escape route into the Valley of Achor.

It is obvious that this is a last-days prophecy because God says that when it is fulfilled, the Jews will call Him "my husband." Currently, the Father and Israel are divorced. That is the primary message of the book of Jeremiah. It is a declaration of divorce (Jer. 3:8).

Israel will remain divorced from God until Jesus returns to earth and establishes the millennial kingdom. The remnant that will be saved will recognize Jesus as the Son of God and the heir to the throne of David forever. All the believing Jews who are alive at the time of Christ's return will be brought to the promised land (Matt. 24:31) and dwell there for the one thousand years and on into the new earth state.

The passage in Hosea 2 describes the millennial kingdom.

1. There will be peace between man and all of nature and its creatures, and everyone will lie down in safety (2:18).
2. God will be betrothed to Israel forever in righteousness and faithfulness (2:19–20).
3. There will be no lack of anything good (2:21–22).

At the time of the book of Hosea, Israel and Judah were divided kingdoms. Jerusalem was the capital of Judah while Samaria was the capital of Israel, the northern kingdom.

The Valley of Achor is the escape route from Jerusalem, not Samaria. So this prophecy is directed to a time where there will be one nation of Israel. That time is now. It is for this reason I said that the passage was a prophecy to all the sons and daughters of Abraham.

A curse turned into a blessing

The Valley of Achor is the location where Joshua had Achan and his family stoned for taking forbidden booty from Jericho (Josh. 7). Achan's sin caused a curse on Israel and a defeat at the hands of the city of Ai after the victory at Jericho, and Joshua named the valley Achor that day.

Achor means "trouble" in Hebrew. What was once a valley of trouble for Israel will become a door of hope during Jacob's Trouble, or the Great Tribulation, which is the last three and a half years of the Tribulation.

God has prepared all the instructions ahead of time for the believing Jews in the Tribulation. Amazingly, Satan is also aware of these instructions, but he will not be able to do anything about it.

15
Two Gospels

> And this gospel of the kingdom shall be preached
> in the whole world for a witness to all the nations,
> and then the end shall come. (Matt. 24:14)

I was reading an article about Anne Graham Lotz's eulogy for her father's (Billy Graham) funeral. The article said that Anne had discovered that the day Billy died was on the day that the Jews remembered Moses's death, February 21. She said that it could be a sign of end-times in that when Moses died, Joshua came after, and the name Joshua is the same in Hebrew as Jesus, or Yeshua. Actually, it is not the same. Jesus is a Greek name, but that is another story. (You can read the article at this link: https://www.wnd.com/2018/03/graham-daughter-sees-significance-in-fathers-death-date/.)

She said perhaps God is telling the church that Jesus is about to return because her father could be a type of Moses. This is my understanding of the point she was trying to make. She said that her father was a great liberator as Moses was, and Joshua was the one who lead Israel into the promised land.

So perhaps her father, she intimated, being called out of this earth, will be replaced by Jesus who will lead the church into heaven.

She then capped her point by saying that Jesus said this: "When the gospel is preached to the whole world as it is today in this service, as it is through churches, missionaries, ministries, Jesus said in Matthew 24:14, 'When the gospel is preached, then the end will come.'"

So the question is, is this a correct interpretation of what Jesus said? Most Christians, in my experience, would agree with Mrs. Lotz. The conventional thinking is that technology and missionaries have enabled the gospel to reach everywhere, and so it is a sign that we are at the end. I do like the analogy of Moses and Joshua, but unfortunately, Billy's daughter is incorrect in her interpretation of Matthew 24:14.

There are two messages labeled as gospel in the New Testament. There is the gospel of the kingdom as labeled by Jesus in Matthew 24 (and John the Baptist in Matthew 3:2), and there is the gospel of salvation as labeled by Paul in Ephesians 1:13.

> In Him, you also, after listening to the message of truth, the gospel of your salvation—having also believed, you were sealed in Him with the Holy Spirit of promise.

There are similarities between the two, but the distinctions between them are critical when it comes to understanding what Matthew 24:14 is talking about and when it takes place.

The similarities are that they are both good news because that is what gospel means. They both are meant to cause people to repent or turn their hearts and lives back to God. And both are soul-saving messages requiring faith with Jesus as the focal point.

The difference in the messages, while nuanced, is significant. One message is the good news of the kingdom of God about to be established on earth, and the other is the good news of the redemption of man. One is about the restoration of God's kingdom on earth with Jesus ruling from Jerusalem, and the other, the restoration of man to God.

Before you go any further, you should read my article in part 3, "The Covert Mission of Jesus Christ." Understanding what Christ's mission was is critical to understanding the gospel of the kingdom.

Again, the gospel of salvation is the message that if you accept Jesus as your Lord and Savior, then your sin will be removed for eternity, and you will become a child of God (a person is not a child of God until they do this [John 1:12]).

In Matthew 24, Jesus is NOT talking to the church. He is talking to the Jews. This is the context. Matthew 24 is mostly about the seventieth week of Daniel, or the seven years of Tribulation. In verse 14, Jesus is describing the spreading of the message of the imminent restoration of the kingdom of God on earth before He returns. Most likely, this is going to happen primarily due to the witnessing work of the 144,000 in Revelation 7 and the two witnesses in Revelation 11.

To reiterate, Jesus is talking to Jews. His intention in Matthew 24 is to leave a survival manual of sorts for the remnant of Israel. That is why He said this in Matthew 24:15, the very next verse: "When you see the ABOMINATION OF DESOLATION which was spoken of through Daniel the prophet, standing in the holy place [let the reader understand], then let those who are in Judea flee to the mountains."

The holy place is the holy of holies in the coming new temple in Jerusalem. This is a message specifically for the Jews to save a Jewish remnant.

The end that Jesus is referring to is the end of the seven-year Tribulation. All the 144,000 and the two witnesses will be killed during the first three and a half years. Then the Great Tribulation (Big T) will begin (Matt. 24:21; Dan. 12:1), which will be the focused destruction of all the Jews and Israel by Satan (Rev. 12) that will last another three and a half years (Dan. 12:7).

The message that was preached before Christ died was the gospel of the kingdom, meaning the kingdom of God is at hand. It will be the same message preached during the seven years of Tribulation.

The first coming, Jesus had to die, which deferred the literal restoration until Jesus returns to earth. The mysteries of the kingdom are here now in the church through the Holy Spirit. But the literal kingdom with Jesus on the throne in Jerusalem for His one-thousand-year reign has not begun.

The message preached now until the Rapture is the gospel of salvation. It could only be preached after Christ died and rose. All mankind has been atoned for (see "What God Has Cleansed" in part 3).

Now to be reconciled to God, a person only must believe in Jesus as his or her Lord and Savior. Repent, turn to Him and denounce sin, and accept Him into your heart and you will become a new creature. You will be forever bound to God through the Holy Spirit, who will never leave you or forsake you (Eph. 1:13–14). Both messages are good news but for different times.

16
The One Who Endures to the End

> But the one who endures to the end, he shall be
> saved. (Matt. 24:13)

This post is a companion piece to the previous chapter, "Two Gospels." After finishing the previous article, I looked a little longer at Matthew 24 and realized it is important to dig further into the context to better understand what Jesus is talking about with regard to "this gospel of the kingdom" in verse 14.

What I have concluded is that there are actually three gospels in the New Testament. There are two gospels of the kingdom and one gospel of redemption. As always, context is the key.

Jesus said that whoever endures to the end shall be saved. He was not talking about the salvation of the soul. He was referring to the survival of the Jewish elect during the Tribulation! Right before Jesus said what He did about enduring to the end, He said that the righteous will be delivered up and be killed and that the love of most will grow cold. What Jesus is saying is that only a few will survive, and He tells them (the Jews) what and how to do it in the next passages.

He tells them to flee into the surrounding hills of Judea when the Antichrist declares himself to be God in the holy place (Matt. 24:15; 2 Thess. 2:4; Dan. 9:27). Then He tells them to stay put when they hear that the Christ has come (Matt. 24:22–26) because it will be gloriously obvious when He does come to earth (Matt. 24:27–30).

This gospel is for the elect Jews, but it is also for every person who gets saved throughout the earth after the Rapture. These are believers who will be enduring the sufferings of the Tribulation. This is the context.

The point is, verse 13 is the good news that Jesus is referring to in verse 14. But it is not about the salvation of the soul; it is about surviving and entering the millennial kingdom that Jesus is going to reign over. The Greek word for *endures* (*hupomeno*) literally means "to survive."

The first gospel of the kingdom preached before Jesus was killed was simply that the Messiah had come and to therefore repent and turn our hearts to God because Jesus was about to reclaim earth and establish His kingdom. I believe that message was a diversion (see "The Covert Mission of Jesus Christ" in part 3).

The second gospel of the kingdom in Matthew 24 is essentially for those who become believers during the Tribulation. The good news is that if you survive, you will live in the righteous kingdom on earth and never die. This is the context of Matthew 24, particularly verses 9–14. When Jesus says "this message" of good news in verse 14, He is referring to the message of verse 13. If you become a believer after the Rapture and you can endure to the end of the Tribulation, you will enter the millennial kingdom on earth and never die.

17
The Gog-Magog War Is Armageddon

I was listening to a podcast by Dr. Michael Heiser on Ezekiel 38 and 39. You can find it on his website nakedbiblepodcast.com. Heiser asserts that the Gog-Magog war takes place at the end of the millennial kingdom. He puts this war in Revelation 20:7. I disagree.

I will make the case that the Gog-Magog war of Ezekiel 38–39 is the final battle when Jesus returns as prophesied in Revelation 19 (which is the same battle mentioned in Revelation 16:14,16). It is not my intention to try and determine who Gog and Magog are. They are from the north; that is all we can say conclusively.

I agree with many things that Heiser teaches. His knowledge and understanding of ancient Hebrew and other ancient languages is immense, to say the least. But I think this issue is pretty simple, and I believe Dr. Heiser, respectfully, is incorrect. Let's start in Ezekiel 36.

Here, God tells Ezekiel to prophesy to Israel that God is going to bring Israel back into the land that He gave to them and cleanse them and give them a new heart and remove the heart of stone from them. This cleansing is key because I do not believe this is talking about the regathering that has taken place up to now. Ezekiel is talking about a second regathering as prophesied in Isaiah 11:11 and Matthew 24:31 that occurs after Jesus physically returns to earth.

Read Ezekiel 36:22–38. This describes a time that does not exist now. ALL the Jews will be back in the promised land, and they will be cleansed, holy, and following the Lord with a new heart, being careful to observe all of God's statutes and ordinances. Does this describe Israel today? No. Israel is a secular nation with a heart of stone as described in Ezekiel 36:26.

Why is this important? Because if the battle takes place at the end of the millennial kingdom, as Heiser asserts, Israel would not be described as having been profaning God's name among the nations (Ezek. 36:22–23).

Moreover, the passage mentioned above describes how all the other nations will know that the Lord is with Israel. If the Gog-Magog war takes place at the end of the millennial kingdom as Heiser believes, then the new earth and eternal state would follow it.

Does the passage in Ezekiel 36 describe the new eternal state after the Lord has created a new earth as written in Revelation 21? No, it does not. There will be no nations in the eternal state, and there will be no state of Israel. There will only be the kingdom of God in the New Jerusalem on a new earth.

Ezekiel 37 continues on to prophesy about the future of Israel in the millennial kingdom. Again, it is not about the first regathering of Israel, which occurred in the last century and ongoing up until now. The way to know this is in the passages.

Ezekiel 37:21–28 once again clearly describes a scenario that is not present today: Israel will no longer follow any other gods, and they will live in ALL the land that was promised to Abraham and Jacob. The Son of David will be ruling, and His sanctuary will be permanent.

This has not happened yet. It will happen when Jesus returns to earth after the seven-year Tribulation, and it will be an immediate and complete regathering (Matt. 24:31). And again, it does not describe the eternal state of Revelation 21.

Ezekiel 38–39 are recapitulations. They are a way of explaining things by reversing and going back over what has been said already but with greater or different details. Here, God tells Ezekiel to prophesy about the Gog-Magog war, which happens right before what has been prophesied in Ezekiel 36 and 37.

At the time of this war, there is a regathered nation of Israel that exists. God is going to bring Gog up against Israel. But it is not the Israel that God describes in Ezekiel 39:22–29, the Israel of the millennial kingdom. It is the Israel with a heart of stone that exists today. This is the conclusion of the war.

"And the house of Israel will know that I am the Lord their God from that day onward. And the nations will know that the house of Israel went into exile for their iniquity because they acted treacherously against Me, and I hid My face from them; so I gave them into the hand of their adversaries, and all of them fell by the sword. According to their uncleanness and according to their transgressions I dealt with them." Therefore, thus says the Lord God, "Now I shall restore the fortunes of Jacob, and have mercy on the whole house of Israel; and I shall be jealous for My holy name. And they shall forget their disgrace and all their treachery which they perpetrated against Me when they live securely on their own land with no one to make them afraid. When I bring them back from the peoples and gather them from the lands of their enemies, then I shall be sanctified in them in the sight of the many nations. Then they will know that I am the Lord their God because I made them go into exile among the nations, and then gathered them again into their own land; and I will leave none of them there any longer. And I will not hide My face from them any longer, for I shall have poured out My Spirit on the house of Israel', declares the Lord God." (Ezek. 39:22–29)

Clearly, this describes a regathered Israel that does not exist today. The Israel of today is the rejected Israel that does not recognize Jesus as the Messiah. The Israel described above is the purged and cleansed Israel that will enter the millennial kingdom.

The second regathering of Israel is that of the angels (Matt. 24:31) when Jesus returns to save the elect, the righteous Jews who survive the Tribulation and recognize Jesus as Messiah. The nations will see and know that the King of Kings is in Zion.

Also, notice in this passage in the second to the last verse above that God says He will bring all the Jews into the land again and that none will be outside of Israel after the regathering.

This confirms that it is talking about a second regathering that immediately precedes the millennial kingdom, and it happens after the war, not before. The first regathering does not include all the Jews, which is the situation now.

Another reason we can know that this battle is right before the return of the Lord and not at the end of the millennial kingdom is through Ezekiel 38:16. It says that this will take place in the last days. That does not refer to the last days of the millennial kingdom. "Last days" or "latter days" always refers to the end of time before the Lord returns to earth and restores His kingdom.

Also, the great supper of God in Revelation 19 and the great sacrifice of God are the same. In Ezekiel 39:17–20, God tells Ezekiel to declare something.

> "And as for you, son of man," thus says the Lord God, "Speak to every kind of bird and to every beast of the field, Assemble and come, gather from every side to My sacrifice which I am going to sacrifice for you, as a great sacrifice on the mountains of Israel, that you may eat flesh and drink blood. So, you will eat fat until you are glutted, and drink blood until you are drunk, from My sacrifice which I have sacrificed for you. And you will be glutted at My table with horses and charioteers, with mighty men and all the men of war, declares the Lord God."

Now read Revelations 19:17–21. Remember, Ezekiel said this was the last days and that it is in connection with the complete restoration of Israel and rule by the Lord Jesus in the millennial kingdom.

> And I saw one standing in the sun; and he cried out with a loud voice, saying to all the birds

which fly in mid-heaven, "Come, assemble for
the great supper of God; in order that you may
eat the flesh of kings and the flesh of command-
ers and the flesh of mighty men and the flesh of
horses and of those who sit on them and the flesh
of all men, both free men and slaves, and small
and great."

The similarities in these passages cannot be dismissed. Both take
place after the battle. I believe that the one referred to in Revelation
19:17 is Ezekiel and not an angel. Yes, the word is *aggelos* or angel,
but it literally just means messenger or "one sent." Every translation
makes this word *angel*, but I believe the messenger in this case will be
Ezekiel because the commandment to speak this herald to the birds
and beasts in Ezekiel 39 was given to him.

I agree with Heiser that this battle will be on Mount Zion. You
will have to listen to his podcast or even read his book *The Unseen
Realm*. It is a great read and gives fantastic insight into the spiritual realm. He explains why Armageddon is Har-magedon, which is
Mount of Assembly and not the Valley of Megiddo. He also summarizes it in the podcast, which I provided the link for above.

During this battle, there will be a great earthquake. It will be
the mother of all earthquakes. This earthquake, according to Ezekiel
38:19, will be so massive it will literally cause the mountains to collapse. Revelation concurs, saying that it will be the largest earthquake since man was created (Rev. 16:18). According to this verse,
Jerusalem will be split into three parts. Every nation will feel it, and
all the mountains on earth will topple. Isaiah 2:2 says that "in the last
days, the mountain of the house of the Lord will be established as the
chief of the mountains, and will be raised above the hills."

This does not occur at the end of the millennial kingdom but
in the last days. The passage goes on to say that "all the nations will
stream" to the mountain of the house of the Lord to be taught. This
is not the eternal new earth as Dr. Heiser's position would dictate.
There will be no nations in the eternal kingdom.

Then all the nations will know that God has won this battle (Ezek. 38:16, 20, 23; 39:7, 21) because they will see Jesus coming in the clouds to earth with His army to save Jerusalem (Rev. 1:7).

After the victory, the house of Israel will be cleaning up the litter of the battle and disposing of the bodies for seven months (Ezek. 39:12). It is another proof that this takes place at the end of the age before Jesus returns, not the end of the millennial kingdom. The cleanup at the end of the millennial kingdom is performed by the Lord Himself when He burns up everything and creates a new heaven and earth (2 Pet. 3:10).

Finally, Revelation 20:7-9 says Satan will be released from prison briefly at the end of the one thousand year kingdom and he will deceive the nations and gather them with Gog and Magog. This is probably the primary passage that Heiser is considering for his assertion that Armageddon takes place at the end of the Millennial Kingdom. But this is not a battle.

This is a crucial point. Armageddon is a battle, but Revelation 20:7-9 is not. It is just a gathering and a surrounding of Jerusalem. This uprising is ended in one fell swoop by God sending down fire and devouring the entire army that Satan has gathered. There is absolutely nothing left of them. The verse says they are "devoured"— totally consumed! There is nothing to bury or clean up, and nothing for the birds to feast on.

18
Why Satan Is Intent on Destroying Israel (and All the Jews)

> And when the dragon saw that he was thrown down to the earth, he persecuted the woman who gave birth to the male child. (Rev. 12:13)

> And the dragon was enraged with the woman, and went off to make war with the rest of her offspring, who keep the commandments of God and hold to the testimony of Jesus. (Rev. 12:17)

Part of the sequence of events that we see consistently in Scripture is the escape and hiding of a remnant of believing Jews in the second half of the Tribulation. Jesus teaches and warns about it in Matthew 24. It is prophesied in Jeremiah 31:1–2, Zechariah 14:5, Hosea 2:14–15, and Revelation 12:6. Revelation 12:13 and 12:17 describe a deliberate and focused attempt to destroy this remnant of elect Jews.

These Jews are believers. They have come to a saving knowledge in Jesus as the Lord and promised Messiah. And Satan is bent on their annihilation. He attempts to destroy every believer during the Tribulation (Rev.13:15), but there is something unique about his desire for the destruction of the Jews.

> O Jerusalem, Jerusalem, who kills the prophets and stones those who are sent to her! How often I

wanted to gather your children together, the way
a hen gathers her chicks under her wings, and
you were unwilling. Behold, your house is being
left to you desolate! For I say to you, from now on
you shall not see Me until you say, "BLESSED IS
HE WHO COMES IN THE NAME OF THE
LORD!" (Matt. 23:37–39)

Jesus is prophesying in the passage above. He is declaring that
the house of Israel has been rejected by Him because they have
rejected Him. And then He says that until the Jews (not just a hand-
ful of disciples) recognize Jesus as the Messiah and Lord, Jesus will
not return. They will not see Him again until then.

Remember Daniel 12 from chapter 11, "Are Travel and
Technology a Last-Days Bible Prophecy?" Daniel is told by the
pre-incarnate Christ (Dan. 10:5–6) that during this period of Great
Tribulation (Dan. 12:1, Matt. 24:21), or the last half of the seven-year period, that many Jews will turn to Christ.

And those who have insight will shine brightly
like the brightness of the expanse of heaven, and
those who lead the many to righteousness, like
the stars forever and ever. (Dan. 12:3)

This is a key piece of the puzzle. We see the same sequence
of events over and over. Daniel 12:1 speaks of Jacob's Distress or
Jacob's Trouble as described by Jeremiah 30:7. Daniel says it is a
time of "distress as never occurred since there was a nation until
that time."

Jesus calls this second half of the Tribulation the Great
Tribulation (Matt. 24:21). It is focused specifically on Israel and the
Jews.

Daniel hears an angel ask the Son of Man in chapter 12 verse
6 how long this period is going to last: "And one said to the man
dressed in linen, who was above the waters of the river, 'How long
will it be until the end of these wonders?'"

The Lord then does something quite significant. He raises both of His hands to heaven, and He swears by the Ancient of Days that it will last a time, times, and a half a time. This is so important that the Son of God swears an oath with both hands to the Father in heaven that it will last three and a half years. This information is that critical.

God put this promise in writing and sealed it with an oath by Himself in front of witnesses so that all the elect Jews, the remnant, would understand how long it would last, that they might obey His warning to stay put in the wilderness until they see Jesus coming in the clouds. This is part of the knowledge that is referred to in Daniel 12:4.

Remember, also, the Feast of Trumpets in the chapter "Jubilee." The informed remnant will have discovered how long the second half of the Tribulation is. They will count the days, and they will probably be listening for the trumpet blast to signal them to prepare for Jesus's return.

The reason Satan is desperate to destroy all the Jews is because if there are no descendants of Abraham, then God would be found a liar, and Jesus would not return. Jesus told the Jews that He would not come again until they say, "BLESSED IS HE WHO COMES IN THE NAME OF THE LORD." This phrase is a Messianic herald from Psalms 118:26.

If there are no Jews to proclaim it, Jesus would not return. This is the motive of the evil one. This is his last-ditch plan to save himself and the earth for his domain. And this is why Jesus was emphatic when He said in Matthew 24:22, "And unless those days had been cut short, no life would have been saved; but for the sake of the elect those days shall be cut short."

19
Every Eye Will See Him

And then the sign of the Son of Man will appear in the sky, and then all the families of the earth will mourn, and they will see the Son of Man coming on the clouds of the sky with power and great glory. (Matt. 24:30)

Behold, He is coming with the clouds, and every eye will see Him, even those who pierced Him; and all the families of the earth will mourn over Him. Even so. Amen. (Rev. 1:7)

And I saw heaven opened; and behold, a white horse and He who sat upon it is called Faithful and True, and in righteousness He judges and wages war. And His eyes are a flame of fire, and upon His head are many diadems; and He has a name written upon Him which no one knows except Himself. And He is clothed with a robe dipped in blood; and His name is called the Word of God. And the armies which are in heaven, clothed in fine linen, white and clean, were following Him on white horses. (Rev. 19:11–14)

God says that when Jesus returns to earth, every human being will see Him as the firmament rips open and He appears in the Shekinah Glory. His army will be surrounding Him, filling the sky with all the hosts of heaven and the raptured church on white horses. He will be coming down to Jerusalem, so His descent will start at meridian over that city. It will be a spectacle that words cannot even begin to effectively describe. The question is, how will every eye be able to see Him?

If Jesus descends over Jerusalem, how will those on the continents of North and South America see Him since they are on the other side of the globe? Does anyone ever think about this? What kind of imaginings must one come up with to answer this question?

I have heard some say that everyone will be able to see it on television. This really does not even merit a response. Do you really believe that God is going to relegate the most dramatic entrance in the history of creation to television?

Or maybe He will not descend from over Israel. Maybe He will start out over Argentina and then do a tour of the world with His entourage until He winds up in Jerusalem. You know, kind of like Santa Claus. No, there will be no whirlwind world tour. He will be coming with urgency to save the elect (Matt. 24:22).

I believe that most people who have even thought about this just think that God is going to supernaturally allow everyone to see the same thing. In other words, God is going to either use a kind of Jedi hypnosis and trick everyone into thinking they are seeing it, like a vision, or He is going to have a cosmic set of mirrors in place that will create a type of reflection or illusion of the real thing. There is no scriptural basis to take any of these scenarios seriously.

The great event will be immediately prefaced by the entire world going under sudden darkness (Matt. 24:29). The sun and moon will black out, and stars will fall. Everything will go silent, and all the attention will be on the sky. Are you picturing the introduction of the home team at an NBA basketball game? Multiply that times a billion.

A mammoth shofar or maybe millions of shofars unseen in the heavens will begin to blow, and then everyone at the same time will see the expanse (hint: *raqiya* [Gen.1:6]) tear apart and the King of Kings appear in glory.

There is only one plausible way that this spectacular event can be seen by every person on earth together when it happens. Do you know what it is? Let him who has ears to hear, hear, and let him who has eyes to see, see.

20
Seventy-Five Days

> And from the time that the regular sacrifice is
> abolished, and the abomination of desolation is
> set up, there will be 1290 days.
>
> How blessed is he who keeps waiting and
> attains to the 1335 days! (Dan. 12:11–12)

Daniel 12 is an amazing chapter. God reveals some incredibly significant information regarding Jesus's post-return. The context of this chapter is Jacob's Trouble, or Great Tribulation, which is the last three and a half years of the seven-year Tribulation period. Verse 1 says it will be a "time of distress such as never occurred since there was a nation."

In verse 6, one of the angels standing by asks the Man in linen, the pre-incarnate Christ, how long until the end of these wonders, or astonishing events. The Man then raises both hands and swears an oath by the throne of Heaven. This is how important the answer is! He says that it will last a time, times, and a half of time (three and a half years) from the time when the Antichrist shatters the power of the holy people.

This shattering of power refers to Daniel 9:27 and the cessation of the sacrificing. When the sacrifices are stopped and the Antichrist declares himself to be God, then all the power has been taken from the Jews, or shattered. The power will then belong to Antichrist. Revelation 13:5–8 says that authority is given to him to rule for forty-two months, which is three and a half years. This will happen in the middle of the seven years.

Daniel heard the Man's answer and oath, but he still did not quite understand. He asks the Lord another question, "What will be the outcome of these events?" Or to put it another way—"Then what?" The Son of Man provides a cryptic answer. He says there will be another seventy-five days.

We know that a time, times, and a half of time is three and a half years. A year on the Hebrew calendar is 360 days, so three and a half years would be 1,260 days. But in verses 11 and 12, He says there will be 1,290 days from the abomination of desolation and then another forty-five days after that. And blessed are the ones who reach 1,335 days.

The question is, what happens during these seventy-five days after Christ sets foot on the Mount of Olives and wins the battle of Har-magedon? We can draw an educated conclusion. I believe the Bible suggests two things.

There will be survivors of the seventieth week of Daniel all over the world. They will include the righteous and unrighteous, and they will be gathered up and brought to the new capital of earth, Jerusalem (Matt. 25:31–32). Then there will be the separation of the sheep from the goats, the wheat from the tares. Matthew 13:40–42 describes this: "The Son of Man will send forth His angels, and they will gather out of His kingdom all stumbling blocks, and those who commit lawlessness, and will cast them into the furnace of fire; in that place there shall be weeping and gnashing of teeth." This is describing hell, not the lake of fire (see the next chapter, "Judgment Day"). The goats and tares will be cast into hell to await destruction at the end of the millennial kingdom.

Interestingly, in the very next verse, Matthew 13:43, Jesus quotes Daniel 12:3: "Then THE RIGHTEOUS WILL SHINE FORTH AS THE SUN in the kingdom of their Father. He who has ears to hear, let him hear."

Daniel 7:9–12 describes this event of the separation. Chapter 7 verse 10 says that myriads upon myriads will stand before the throne of the Ancient of Days. We know this is not the Great White Throne Judgment of Revelation 20 because Daniel 7:12 says the "rest of the beasts" are granted an "extension of life for an appointed time."

If this was the Great White Throne Judgment that takes place at the end of the millennial kingdom, then Satan, the false prophet and Antichrist, would be cast into the lake of fire for eternity. There would be no extension of life. At this judgment, the separation, the wicked will be killed and sent to hades; and to the righteous, He will say, "Well done, enter into the joy of your King."

So this is probably the reason for the seventy-five days Jesus declares in Daniel 12. Those who make it to day 1,335 are indeed blessed. I must think that after all the gathering and separating has taken place, on day 1,335, there will be a celebration that defies imagination. Jesus will be on His throne, reigning over the earth on Mount Zion (Mic. 4:7, Zech. 8:3). What a day that will be.

21
Judgment Day

The Bible simply does not teach that the lost sinner will spend eternity in unimaginable pain and torment in a raging inferno. It teaches that every person is born doomed to destruction unless they receive Jesus Christ as their Savior. I will demonstrate both points.

When a person receives Jesus, they receive eternal life. There are no passages that say an unbeliever will spend eternity in hell or fire. If they do not obey the gospel of salvation, then they will wait in hell until the Great White Throne Judgment of Revelation 20 and be thrown into the lake of fire and destroyed. The idea of eternal suffering in hell is a conclusion based on flawed hermeneutics, or method of interpretation.

The opposite of eternal life is eternal death

> God so loved the world that He gave His only begotten Son, that whoever believes in Him shall not PERISH, but have ETERNAL LIFE. (John 3:16)

> These [(1 Thess 1:8)] will pay the penalty of eternal DESTRUCTION, away from the presence of the Lord and from the glory of His power. (2 Thess. 1:8-9)

This position is called conditionalism. In other words, eternal life is conditional. Mankind is not born into immortality. We are born doomed unless we accept Jesus Christ. This is obeying the gospel of our Lord Jesus.

If you obey the gospel by repenting and accepting Christ as your Savior and Lord, then you receive the GIFT of eternal life. If you do not, then you will be destroyed. Eternal destruction does not mean that you are slowly destroyed for eternity. That is ridiculous. It means that you are destroyed and that there is no undoing. The destruction is eternal, no coming back; you will no longer exist.

There are a few critical points that must be understood.

1. Hell is not the lake of fire.
2. The lake of fire is also known as Gehenna.
3. Hell/hades is a waiting place for the Great White Throne Judgment.
4. Hades/hell will be destroyed in the lake of fire prior to the eternal state.
5. Hades and hell are the same.

In the story of the rich man and Lazarus (Luke 16:23), the rich man has died and gone to hades where he is in torment. This is hell. It is hot, and there is no water. This is where all the lost go until the Great White Throne Judgment.

Hell is not the lake of fire

Revelation 20:14 says that hades is thrown into the lake of fire and destroyed. They cannot be the same. Hades is thrown in with death. We know that death will be destroyed. First Corinthians 15:26 says that the last enemy to be destroyed is death. Hades will be destroyed with it. They are not going to be slowly consumed but never totally for eternity. Neither will the lost be slowly consumed but never totally for eternity. That is nonsense, frankly.

The lake of fire is also known as Gehenna

In Mark 9:43–48, Jesus is teaching and says it is better to remove parts of the body that cause you to stumble rather than keep them and be cast into Gehenna. If your Bible says "hell," that is a mistransliteration. The Greek is "Gehenna."

Gehenna is a derivative of words that mean "Valley of Hinnom." It was literally the garbage dump outside of Jerusalem where a constant fire was burning to consume all the refuse including dead carcasses. This is not synonymous with hell. The constant consuming fire is the lake of fire where everything thrown in will be consumed (except Satan, the beast and false prophet [Rev. 20:10]).

Jesus said, "Do not fear those who can kill the body but are unable to kill the soul, but fear Him who can destroy the body and soul in Gehenna" (Matt. 10:28). Again, if your Bible says "hell" instead of "Gehenna," that is another mistransliteration.

There are a couple of ways to understand this verse, both end up with the unsaved being destroyed. How to understand it depends on whether you understand Revelation 20:5 to mean that the unsaved receive a body when they "come to life."

In Revelation 20:5, it says that the first resurrection (at the end of the Tribulation) are the righteous who died during the Tribulation. Blessed are those who participate in that. The rest of the dead (unsaved) do not come to life until after the one-thousand-year kingdom.

If they just come to life and do not receive a body, then the verse would be understood this way: "But fear him who can destroy the body, and destroy the soul in Gehenna." If they do receive another fleshly body, then it would be easier to understand it as to "destroy the body and soul."

It does seem to make more sense that they would receive a body, especially the way Matthew 10:28 is written. It says man can KILL the body but that God can DESTROY the body and soul in Gehenna. Plus, they are already alive in hell, so to say they will "come to life" seems inappropriate and redundant unless the meaning is some type of regeneration of the old body.

The point either way is they will be destroyed in Gehenna, the lake of fire. This is the second death in Revelation 20:14. The first death is the death of the body, and the second death is the death of the soul—eternal destruction.

Hell/hades is a waiting place for the lost until the Great White Throne Judgment. Refer to the story of Lazarus and the rich man. The rich man was not in the lake of fire; he was in hades. He will be judged and destroyed at the great judgment. Revelation 20:13 says that hades will give up the dead that are in it, and then they will be judged and thrown into the lake of fire.

Revelation 14:9–11 is not talking about eternal torment in hell or lake of fire. This is a passage used quite often to prove eternal torment of the lost. It is saying no such thing. Read it carefully. To make it say eternal torment for the lost, you must insert the meaning; you cannot take it out of it.

> And another angel, a third one, followed them, saying with a loud voice, 'If anyone worships the beast and his image, and receives a mark on his forehead or upon his hand, he will also drink of the wine of the wrath of God, which is mixed in full strength in the cup of His anger; and he will be tormented with fire and brimstone in the presence of the holy angels and in the presence of the Lamb.
>
> And the smoke of their torment goes up forever and ever; and they have no rest day and night, those who worship the beast and his image, and whoever receives the mark of his name.

The people who take this mark and worship the beast think that this is going to make their lives easy (Rev. 13:17). God says it is going to be just the opposite. In other words, this is describing a terrible hardship doled out by God in the last days of the Tribulation. I believe the purpose of the torment may be to get these people to repent before it is too late.

What the eternal torment supporters will say is that this verse says they will be tormented forever. It says no such thing. It says they will drink of the wrath of God in full strength. The context here is while they are alive on the earth. Keep reading the passage and go to verses 18–19.

> And another angel, the one who has power over fire, came out from the altar; and he called with a loud voice to him who had the sharp sickle, saying "Put in your sharp sickle, and gather the clusters from the vine of the earth, because her grapes are ripe."
>
> And the angel swung his sickle to the earth and gathered the clusters from the vine of the earth and threw them into the great wine press of the wrath of God.

The point is that this is describing the wrath of God being poured out on the earth, not the final judgment at the Great White Throne.

The passage in chapter 14 verse 11 says that the smoke of their torment goes up forever and ever. There are two things to consider here: It is the smoke of their torment, and it goes up as far as it can into the eternal heavens. It is describing location and distance, not time.

The original Aramaic says the smoke goes up to the "eternity of eternities." It is NOT saying their torment goes on in time for eternity. The passage does not give liberty to draw that meaning from it. Look at Isaiah 34:9–10. It is talking about God's wrath against the nations and, in this case, Edom.

> And its streams shall be turned into pitch, and its loose earth into brimstone, and its land shall become burning pitch.
>
> It shall not be quenched night or day; it's smoke shall go up forever; from generation to

generation it shall be desolate; none shall pass through it forever and ever.

Clearly, Edom is not smoking today. The smoke going up forever is idiomatic. It is about how high it is going. Also, the passage in Revelation 14 says that these will be tormented in the presence of the Lamb, and they will have no rest. The context is on earth. These are suffering in the presence of God, and God is receiving the smoke. On the contrary, at the great judgment, the lost will "suffer the penalty of eternal destruction <u>AWAY</u> from the presence of the Lord and from the glory of His power."(2 Thess. 1:9) To say that this passage is talking about eternal torment in hell is simply bad exegesis.

Matthew 25:41

Matthew 25:41 is another major verse used to support eternal torment for the lost: "Then He will also say to those on His left, 'Depart from Me, accursed ones, into the eternal fire which has been prepared for the devil and his angels.'"

First, what is this verse NOT saying? It does not say that the accursed will suffer torment for eternity. It just says they will be cast into the eternal fire. We know the eternal fire is Gehenna or the lake of fire, not hell/hades. It is the fire that is constantly burning that consumes everything thrown into it. As already pointed out, it is synonymous with the Valley of Hinnom, which is the garbage dump that was outside Jerusalem that had the continuous fire (Matt. 10:28).

It also says that the lake of fire is prepared for Satan and his messengers. The Greek word for *angel* is *aggelos*, which means messenger or envoy. Who are Satan's envoys? They are the false prophet and Antichrist. They are Satan's agents or representatives who are to come. According to the verse, these are whom the lake of fire is prepared for. Revelation 20:10 says that, the false prophet and the beast (Antichrist), will be thrown into the lake of fire, and their torment will go on for eternity.

The Bible lists only Satan, the false prophet and Antichrist, as the one who will suffer for eternity in the lake of fire.

Outer darkness

Matthew records three different passages where the unsaved or wicked are cast into the outer darkness where there is weeping and gnashing of teeth: Matthew 8:12, 22:13, and 25:30.

There is nothing in the passages that say this is the lake of fire or eternal torment. A strong enough case has been made that the lake of fire consumes and destroys, so the weeping and gnashing of teeth will not happen there.

I am going to bring in the book of Enoch here. This extrabiblical book is valid spiritual history, and that is how the ancient Hebrew viewed it. One reason I can say it is valid is because the Bible quotes it and references it (Jude 6, 1 Peter 3:19–20, 2 Peter 2:4); therefore, God affirms it. I am not claiming it is God-breathed scripture. In Enoch 22, there is a description of the separation of the places for the unrighteous and righteous dead souls.

> At that time therefore I inquired respecting him, and respecting the general judgment, saying, "Why is one separated from another?" He answered, "Three separations have been made between the spirits of the dead, and thus have the spirits of the righteous been separated.
>
> Namely, by a chasm, by water, and by light above it.
>
> And in the same way likewise are sinners separated when they die and are buried in the earth; judgment not overtaking them in their lifetime.
>
> Here their souls are separated. Moreover, abundant is their suffering until the time of the great judgment, the castigation, and the torment of those who eternally execrate, whose souls are punished and bound there forever."

And thus has it been from the beginning of the world. Thus has there existed a separation between the souls of those who utter complaints, and of those who watch for their destruction, to slaughter them in the day of sinners. (Enoch 22:9–13)

What Enoch is saying is, there are three things that separate the unsaved from the saved who are dead (that was pre-cross; now the saved go straight to heaven, but hell remains the same). There is a chasm, water, and light above the water. (As an aside, Enoch also affirms the destruction of the lost.)

Remember the story of the rich man and Lazarus (Luke 16:19–26)? It says the rich man asked if Lazarus could dip his finger in the water and put it on the rich man's tongue. Abraham said there was a chasm that may not be crossed. Both passages describe the chasm and water.

Jesus is also affirming Enoch in his telling of this story. But the important thing here is that one of the things that the righteous have and the unrighteous do not is light.

I believe the only conclusion is that the outer darkness is hell. It is dark and hot, and there is no water. And there is weeping and gnashing of teeth as they ponder their disobedience to the gospel and their coming judgment at the Great White Throne.

Conditionalism represents the true nature of God

Finally, to understand that the final judgment is eternal death and destruction is to understand the true nature of God. For someone to suffer eternal, unfathomable agony and torture is senseless and cruel. God's justice is righteous, for sure, but it is not maniacal.

What would be the point of eternal torture? It is bad enough that you will not live forever with God. Spending at least one thousand years in hell (or more for the lost who are already dead) knowing you are going to be destroyed for all eternity is pretty dreadful.

22
Outside

> Blessed are those who wash their robes, that they may have the right to the tree of life and may enter by the gates into the city. Outside are the dogs and the sorcerers, and the immoral persons and the murderers and the idolaters, and everyone who loves and practices lying. (Rev. 22:14–15)

On the way home from visiting family, I was listening to a Christian program on the radio. It was one of those Bible answer man shows where people would call in or write with questions. The person who was answering them was from Moody Bible Institute. I recall he had a doctorate in theology.

The subject of the verse is the city New Jerusalem that will come down out of heaven and be the dwelling place for everyone on the new earth. The subject of the question was basically, "What's going on here?" The questioner said it sounded like there are unsaved people on the new earth living outside the gates of the New Jerusalem.

I was really surprised at the answer that the scholar gave. He said that it appeared from the passage that the lake of fire would be within eyesight of the New Jerusalem and that those who are living in the city would be able to see the suffering unsaved burning in the lake. I was kind of shocked at the level of understanding he showed. It was evidence that a ThD does not make you biblically literate.

Before I get into the problems with the doctor's answer and the correct understanding of the passage, make sure you read the previous chapter "The Judgment." If you have not read it or ever considered that the unsaved will be destroyed instead of suffering in unimaginable burning pain for eternity, it will give you the background and support for my response.

I can understand why the radio host responded the way he did. He believes that people will suffer for eternity while burning in the lake of fire. His bias and his programming were what informed him of the passage's meaning. In other words, his incorrect belief led him to conclude that the saved will be able to see the unsaved roasting in the lake of fire.

There are two problems. One is his incorrect understanding of hell and judgment in the Bible. The other problem is his lack of discernment as to the context of the passage. In a nutshell, the context is about spiritual position or condition, not geographic location.

Revelation 22:12 says that Jesus is coming to render to every man according to what he has done. It is a future event. For the saved, it is rewards. For the unsaved, it is destruction. Those who do not obey the gospel of the Lord Jesus Christ (2 Thess. 1:8) will be destroyed away from the presence of the Lord: "And these will pay the penalty of eternal destruction, away from the presence of the Lord" (2 Thess. 1:9).

Revelation 22:14 gives an obvious clue that verse 15 is metaphorical and is talking about spiritual condition rather than geographic location. It says, "Blessed are those who wash their robes, that they may have the <u>RIGHT</u> to the tree of life and <u>MAY</u> enter into the city." The others in verse 15 do not have that right, and they are characterized as outside. They do NOT have the right to enter the city, and they will be thrown into the lake of fire and destroyed.

I would venture to say that the scholar conflated Revelation 22:15 with Matthew 8:12: "The sons of the kingdom shall be cast into the outer darkness; in that place there shall be weeping and gnashing of teeth." My guess is that he believes these verses are saying the same thing. They are not.

Matthew 8 is talking about hell, not the lake of fire. There <u>IS</u> weeping and gnashing of teeth in the darkness and heat of hell as these souls await their judgment at the Great White Throne in

Revelation 20. They will be judged and then destroyed in the lake of fire. Think about it.

If it is outer darkness, then how would anyone from the New Jerusalem be able to see into it? And what would be the purpose of having the lake of fire right by the New Jerusalem and everyone in the city constantly having to view the horrible suffering going on (that is, if anyone was actually suffering in it besides Satan, the Antichrist and false prophet [Rev. 20:10])? It is absurd on its face.

The Greek definition of the word *outside* in Revelation 22:15 is "exo," which does mean outside. Metaphorically, they are outside the city. They are not in the position or have the right to enter into the city that is coming. They are separated from the glory and blessing of salvation. The opposite of inside is outside. In other words, a person can be both destroyed and outside of the city. The point is, they are not IN the city.

We are not going to be subjected to some senseless and cruel eternal spectacle of tormented and suffering souls. Neither will anyone suffer like that for eternity other than Satan, the Antichrist and the false prophet.

23
The Golan Heights Have Always Belonged to Israel

I originally published this article in March of 2019. I am including it in this book to show what the promised land was supposed to encompass and what it will encompass when Jesus returns.

As I am writing this, Israel is firing rockets into the Gaza Strip in retaliation to a rocket attack by Hamas. This comes right on the heels of President Trump signing a formal declaration that the Golan Heights is now Israel land.

It has always been Israel land. In fact, the land that God gave to Abraham and his descendants makes the current borders of Israel look like Vermont compared to Texas. The land that God set aside for the children of Abraham extends from the Nile up to Turkey down through the middle of Iraq to Kuwait and across west through Saudi Arabia back to Egypt and the Nile River.

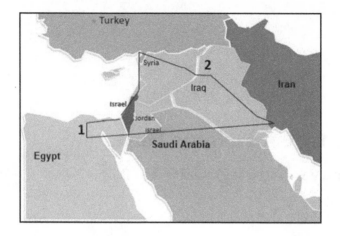

> On that day the Lord made a covenant with
> Abram, saying, "To your descendants I have given
> this land, from the river of Egypt as far as the
> great river, the river Euphrates; the Kenite and
> Kenizzite and the Kadmonite and the Hittite and
> Perizzite and the Rephaim and the Amorite and
> Canaanite and the Girgashite and the Jebusite."
> (Gen. 15:8)

In the illustration above, number 1 is the Nile River (River of
Egypt) and number 2 is the Euphrates River. Israel today is the small
purple nation. All the land between these two rivers as outlined was
given to the children of Israel. This is the space that Israel will occupy
during the millennial kingdom. The promise to Abraham will be
entirely fulfilled when Jesus returns and reigns from Mount Zion.

> And you will know that I am the Lord, when I
> bring you into the land of Israel, into the land
> which I swore to give to your forefathers. (Ezek.
> 20:42)

The biblical landmass granted to Abraham includes approximately two thirds of what is today's Syria. The Golan Heights is a
speck of land between Israel and Syria that Israel captured from Syria

during the Six-Day War in 1967. In 1981, Israel unilaterally annexed this land. Until today, Monday, March 25, no other nation has recognized the Golan Heights as belonging to Israel.

Of course, the anti-Israel, anti-Bible factions are condemning this act by the president as a threat to world order. These condemnations simply give voice to the satanic forces that hate Israel as a symbol of the truth of the Bible and the reality that the God of the Bible is the one true, sovereign Most High God. This is the essence of the political war that is being waged by the nations and the military war that is being built by Islamic terrorist states against Israel.

What happened today is just another warning bell sounding an alarm of the imminent second coming of Jesus Christ. It is a simple reminder that Israel is a focal point of the spiritual war that is raging and that will climax at Armageddon when Jesus returns (Zech. 12:2, 14:2).

24

The Feast of Booths

> On exactly the fifteenth day of the seventh month, when you have gathered in the crops of the land, you shall celebrate the feast of the Lord for seven days, with a sabbath rest on the first day and a sabbath rest on the eighth day. (Lev. 23:39)

> You shall thus celebrate it as a feast to the Lord for seven days in the year. It shall be a perpetual statute throughout your generations; you shall celebrate it in the seventh month. You shall live in booths for seven days; all the native born in Israel shall live in booths. (Lev. 23:41–42)

The Feast of Booths, or Sukkoth, occurs on the Hebrew calendar on the fifteenth of Tishri, which is the seventh month. It is the last feast of the year of the seven feasts designated by God in Leviticus (Lev. 23:1–44). These were God's declared holy convocations and appointed times that the Hebrews were required to observe annually. These feasts ultimately foreshadowed the coming Messiah and His mission.

All the spring feasts (Unleavened Bread, Passover, Firstfruits, and Pentecost) have had fulfillment in Jesus's first coming. The fall feasts (Trumpets, Atonement, and Booths) have yet to be completely fulfilled and will be at Jesus's second coming. I do believe that a partial fulfillment has been accomplished with the Feast of Atonement and the Feast of Booths.

I encourage you to research this subject for yourself. While the feasts were only for the Jews to observe, they are important for Christians to understand. They display God's wisdom and His agenda. I only want to focus on the Feast of Booths in this chapter.

The Feast of Booths is the last fall feast following the Feasts of Trumpets and Atonement in that order. Leviticus says that the purpose of this holy convocation is to remind the Jews every year that God had them live in booths when He brought them out from the land of Egypt (Lev. 23:43).

In Exodus 23:16, it is also called by God as the Feast of Ingathering: "Also, the Feast of Ingathering at the end of the year when you gather in the fruit of your labors from the field" (see also Exod. 34:22).

The question is, why did God want to constantly remind the Jews that He had them live in booths when they left Egypt?

A booth, or sukkah (*cukkah* is the literal Hebrew), was a temporary, meager shelter. It had four sides and roof made with various types of branches from leafy trees (Neh. 8:15). The tradition is that the night sky could be seen through them.

In Genesis 33:17, it says that Jacob journeyed to a place where he built a house for himself and booths for his livestock. The place from that time forward was called Succoth or Sukkot, which means booths.

This question of why God wanted to remind the Jews that He had them live in booths has even greater dimension when you realize that it is the only feast that will be observed by everyone during the millennial kingdom with Jesus reigning from Jerusalem.

> Then it will come about that any who are left of all the nations that went against Jerusalem will go up from year to year to worship the King, the Lord of Hosts, and to celebrate the Feast of Booths. (Zech. 14:16)

When the Hebrews were freed from Egypt, the first place they camped was called Succoth (Exod. 13:20). This was not the same Succoth as Jacob's Succoth.

It is a reasonable assumption that they made booths and lived in them at that location. The reason we must assume it is because it does not say specifically that they did in the passage in Exodus. But Leviticus does specifically say that God had them make and dwell in booths. I would guess that the name of the place came from the fact that they lived in booths there.

To fully understand the Feast of Booths, it is also significant that the Shekinah Glory of God appeared first at Succoth. The pillar of cloud and of fire is first mentioned in this passage.

> And the Lord was going before them in a pillar
> of cloud by day to lead them on the way, and in a
> pillar of fire by night to give them light, that they
> might travel by day and by night. (Exod. 13:21)

So God manifested Himself physically among the Jews.

Will God indeed dwell with mankind on earth?

Coinciding with everything I have mentioned thus far is that Solomon's Temple was dedicated—and the glory of the Lord filled it—during the Feast of Booths.

> And all the men of Israel assembled themselves
> to King Solomon at the feast, in the month of
> Ethanim [Tishri], which is the seventh month.
>   And it came about when the priests came
> from the holy place, that the cloud filled the
> house of the Lord. (1 Kings 8:2, 10)

In 2 Chronicles 6:18, after the glory of the Lord filled the temple, Solomon exclaimed, "But will God indeed dwell with mankind on the earth?"

This was not a question of doubt or ignorance but of wonderment and awe. And we know this occurred during the Feast of Booths because it was one of the three feasts where all the males of Israel had to assemble (Exod. 23:17, Exod. 34:23, Deut. 16:16), 1 Kings 8 says all the men of Israel assembled and it happened in the seventh month.

As mentioned earlier in Zechariah 14:16, the Feast of Booths is the only feast that is required to be observed by all the nations during the millennial reign of Jesus Christ on earth. (According to Ezekiel 45, it appears that the Jews in the millennial kingdom will also observe the Passover.)

Representatives from all the surviving nations will be required to go to Israel and live in booths just as the Jews did before Christ. This means Jews and Gentiles. Any who does not go, that nation will not receive any rain, presumably at least until the next Feast of Booths (Zech. 14:17–18).

Finally, Jesus was born in a booth. He was born in a small shelter for livestock and laid in a feeding trough (manger). And He was born during the Feast of Booths in the fall, not December 25. God came to earth in the form of man during this feast, and He dwelt with man. Therefore, the Feast of Booths has been partially fulfilled as a foreshadowing of the ultimate fulfillment.

There is no specific passage that explains exactly why God commanded the Jews to live in booths for seven days every year. Nor is there a verse that explains why God will require the nations to observe this feast either. But from all the passages mentioned above, we can make an educated conclusion.

I believe the Scriptures express two primary reasons. First, it was instituted to remind the Jews that God was their provider. The feast takes place after the harvest is gathered and is also referred to as the Feast of Ingathering. The Jews celebrated with a great feast but sacrificed their first fruits to the Lord. It reminded the Jews that it was God who brought them out of slavery and cared for them in the wilderness. In the millennial kingdom, the nations will also need to be reminded that the King of Kings is the provider of all the earth.

Interestingly, it is also probably why the forgiveness of debts every seven years happened during the Feast of Booths (Deut. 15:1–2, 31:10). In other words, the forgiveness of debts is an act of faith in the Lord providing.

I think it is important to include that when Jesus returns, there is going to take place the great harvest. As explained in chapter 20, all of the righteous and unrighteous, the wheat and tares, will be gathered for separating. This happens during the Feast of Ingathering, which is the other name for Feast of Booths. This harvest of souls is a fulfillment of The Feast of Ingathering.

Lastly, and maybe most importantly, Sukkot was to teach and remind the Jews that it was God's desire and plan to dwell with man permanently in an eternal kingdom.

Booths and the Tabernacle and Temple were temporary. But God dwelt in all of them. And when Jesus reigns on earth during the millennial kingdom, He will require the feast to be observed because He wants the nations to be reminded that He is seated on the throne in Jerusalem, ruling and dwelling with man. But that also will be a temporary realm.

It is God's burning desire to dwell with man, whom He loves, and provide all good things. He has tarried this longing to return because He wants to live with multitudes upon multitudes of people. When the new heaven and earth are created, there will be no need of any reminders. It will be forever and ever.

25
Gentiles in the Tribulation

There is hope for everyone who goes through the Tribulation. In chapter 15, I explained how the world was going to be reached with the saving message, "Repent for the kingdom of God is coming." This work will be a result primarily of the twelve thousand from each of the twelve tribes of Jacob in Revelation 7 as well as the preaching ministry of the two witnesses in Revelation 11.

I wanted to include this short message because some may think after reading this book that all Bible prophecy is about the Jews. Much of it is because of the promises made to Abraham and his descendants as I have laid out.

In Revelations 7:9, John sees a multitude of people from every nation, tribe, and tongue, and they are clothed in white robes.

All of heaven's angels were standing around the throne with the elders and the four living creatures, and one of the elders asks John if he knew who these people were in the white robes. John said to him, "My lord, you know." In other words, "Please tell me." This was the response of the elder in chapter 7 verse 14.

> And he said to me, "These are the ones who come out of the great tribulation and they have washed their robes and made them white in the blood of the Lamb."

These people in question are people from every ethnic background who turn to Christ as their Savior during the seventieth week of Daniel and are martyred for their faith.

I believe that the greatest period of evangelism will take place during the Tribulation. More people will come to Christ in less time than ever before. As terrible a period it will be, it will result in the salvation of millions. Chapter 7 verse 14 says, "God shall wipe every tear from their eyes." Eternal life will be worth it.

But not every person will die during the Tribulation. Many will survive to populate the earth during the millennial kingdom. After Jesus returns, all the righteous Jews on earth will be gathered into Israel. That is what Matthew 24:31 explains. They will be brought into the promised land to fulfill the promise made to Abraham and his descendants.

The rest of the world will be populated by believing non-Jews. They will make up "the nations" as explained in the previous chapter. All the nations will be required to send representatives to Jerusalem to celebrate the Feast of Booths.

Also, it says in Revelation 20:8 that at the end of the one thousand years, Satan will be allowed free for a brief time. He will deceive the nations and incite many people to rebel. These will be wicked, unbelieving people who will perish at the final rebellion. It is a futile attempt.

The point is that there will be many people who come to Christ during the seven-year Tribulation. There is hope for all until Jesus returns.

PART 3

26
The Covert Mission of Jesus Christ

> But we speak God's wisdom in a mystery, the
> hidden wisdom, which God predestined before
> the ages to our glory; the wisdom which none of
> the rulers of this age has understood; for if they
> had understood it, they would not have crucified
> the Lord of glory. (1Cor. 2:7–8)

The man who never was

The annals of war are replete with stories of subterfuge. In WWII, there were several elaborate schemes designed to fool Hitler about the invasion of Europe. The most exotic ruse of the war took place before the invasion of Italy, the success of which had enormous impact on the coming invasion of France.

Before the Allies could invade France, they had to get a foothold in Southern Europe. Germany had been shoved out of North Africa, and conventional wisdom said the next step for the Allies would be to land an army in Sicily. Germany knew this as well.

Winston Churchill famously remarked that "everyone but a bloody fool would know" that the objective was Sicily. If the Allies could make the Germans believe that they were going to invade Greece instead of Sicily, significant forces might get diverted, thereby ensuring success in Sicily. So a ruse was concocted. The audacious plan became the basis for a film entitled *The Man Who Never Was* in 1956.

The idea, thought up by twenty-five-year-old RAF flight lieutenant Charles Cholmondeley and developed by British intelligence, was to drop a dead body off the coast of Nazi-occupied Spain complete with identification papers, photos of a girlfriend, love letters, a London bus ticket, and most importantly, a personal letter from Lt. General Archibald Nye.

The chosen courier was a deceased thirty-four-year-old alleged homeless man named Glyndwr Michael, who had supposedly been found in an abandoned warehouse. (There is controversy about whether he was a homeless person.) For this mission, designated Operation Mincemeat, he was given the name Capt. William H.N. Martin.

The letter from General Nye outlined several sensitive topics. One of the topics was Allied plans in the Mediterranean, specifically the invasion of Greece. It described plans to embark troops from Egypt and Libya under the command of General Jumbo Wilson for the landing in Greece. It also mentioned a simultaneous landing on Sardinia by forces under the command of General Harold Alexander, at the time in Tunisia. The letter was personally written and signed by General Nye. Nye added the finishing touch in the letter saying, "We stand a very good chance of making the enemy think we are landing in Sicily."

Next, the British had to make the dead man look as if he had drowned. The plan was to make the Germans think the body had washed up from a plane crash at sea. To make the death look as authentic as possible, the British stored the body in dry ice in a sealed container. As the ice evaporated, the lungs filled with liquid.

The body, dressed in Royal Marine battle dress, was found on the shore of Spain near a town called Huelva with the briefcase of papers attached. He had been dropped in the ocean a mile from shore by the submarine HMS *Seraph*. Within days, the contents of the briefcase were in German intelligence hands.

Of course, the Germans would want the British to think that the documents had remained secure so as not to tip the British that the Germans were now in on the Allied plans. So the Germans had the Spanish return the contents just as they had found them. But

British intelligence examined the documents, and they could tell they had been tampered with. The plan was working.

A few days later, German reinforcements were moving to Greece, Corsica, and Sardinia over the objection of Italian dictator Mussolini, who still believed the invasion would be in Sicily. Panzer tank divisions were sent from France and Russia, and Germany's greatest field general, Erwin Rommel, was sent to Greece to command.

The great deception worked magnificently, so much so that two days after the invasion of Sicily, Hitler refused to budge from Greece, believing the main invasion was still to come. How did this ruse affect D-day?

Hitler eventually realized he had been duped at Sicily. Two days after the D-day invasion of France, Germans confiscated documents from a landing craft on the shore of Normandy. The documents were real, and they detailed inland targets of the Allies.

Hitler refused to believe they were real, convinced it was another ruse and that the main invasion was still to come farther north at Pas-de-Calais. When the Germans needed the Panzer divisions the most at Normandy, Hitler kept them frozen inland off the northern coast of France. The invasion of France may well have been saved by the lasting effects of *The Man Who Never Was*.

In a way, Jesus played a "man who never was."

Yahweh, the greatest con artist

God tricked Satan, plain and simple. The Jews were looking for a political and military leader, which was precisely what God took advantage of. Jesus intentionally allowed and even fostered their belief that He had come to restore the kingdom of God on earth.

Jesus executed his mission flawlessly, gathering and training believing followers while conning Satan and the unbelieving Jews. Turning the entire nation of Israel's attention on Himself, He was able to keep His true mission cloaked: to be killed.

Jesus drew crowds of thousands in empty areas near tiny towns and villages. There, He preached messages of hope laced with fiery, revolutionary rhetoric. "The kingdom of God is coming," He said repeatedly. He rebuked, chastised, and humiliated the reigning authorities, the oppressive religious overlords who bowed to the pagan conquerors from Rome.

And God spoke from heaven, and all who were present heard it: "This is My Beloved Son! This is the One sent to restore the kingdom of God back on earth to where it belongs—in the hands of the Messiah King reigning from Jerusalem! This is the One that would throw off the oppressors!"

What was Satan hearing? "The kingdom of God is near"; "The gates of hell will not prevail"; "I saw Satan falling like lightning"; "Do not think that I came to bring peace on the earth. I did not come to bring peace but a sword!"

John the Baptist called them out. "Who warned you of the wrath to come?"

Satan heard what the Pharisees and scribes were hearing: declarations of war and vengeance! The Pharisees were the imagers, the mirrors of Satan. Jesus called them sons of Satan. How they reacted was how Satan was reacting. Their authority and power were threatened as were Satan's power and authority as ruler of this domain earth.

The hook was set. Jesus had to die. He spoke in parables for the ears that could hear. He knew that only a very few were understanding any of what he said. He knew the crowds would turn on him. But he also knew that in the end, He would find the few followers who would commit their lives to Him.

The mission was to die. But it was also to lay the foundation for the church. He made sure that His disciples knew He was God in the flesh. He trained them how to become fishers of men. He taught them the message of salvation and how to spread it, to love one another and to live for eternity.

He did this, all the while provoking Satan with impending overthrow of his reign on earth. And Yahweh chose the perfect time to insert His Son into the world. Knowing He would be rejected, He rightfully claimed the throne of David. But it was never His intent to take it at that time. His intent was to be killed.

It was a brilliant plan, laid out in Eden and flawlessly managed all the way to the cross. From the beginning of creation, it was determined. Yahweh would restore man and earth back to Himself by sending His Son to die. And He rose from the dead to seal the victory. Satan would not have laid a finger on Him had he understood Jesus's real mission.

27
What God Has Cleansed

> And on the next day, as they were on their way, and approaching the city, Peter went up on the housetop about the sixth hour to pray. And he became hungry and was desiring to eat; but while they were making preparations, he fell into a trance; and he beheld the sky opened up, and a certain object like a great sheet coming down, lowered by four corners to the ground, and there were in it all kinds of four-footed animals and crawling creatures of the earth and birds of the air. And a voice came to him, "Arise, Peter, kill and eat!" But Peter said, "By no means, Lord, for I have never eaten anything unholy and unclean." And again, a voice came to him a second time, "What God has cleansed, no longer consider unholy." (Acts 10:9–15)

Here is an example of a viewpoint or interpretation I have always accepted as true without really studying it out. I believe many Christians are in a similar position.

I was listening to an interview with a Christian couple who are involved in Biblical dieting. They were remarking about this passage and said that it has nothing to do with God saying everything is okay to eat now. They pointed out that Peter realized that the vision was telling him that he should not call any man unclean or unholy. The couple said that it was never in the law for a Jew to view people this way.

I have always accepted the contention that in this passage, God says that all animals are now okay to eat and that God's law that forbade certain animals was now nullified. It was then somehow equated symbolically to the notion that Jews could also now associate with non-Jews. In other words, we are not under the law any longer.

So I decided to study all this for myself. I found that the aforementioned couple was correct. However, they did not complete the picture. There was something much deeper and more profound that God was communicating to Peter.

Peter goes into a trance and sees a vision. A great sheet comes down from heaven, and all kinds of unclean and unholy (dirty and impure) animals are in the sheet. A voice tells Peter to arise, kill, and eat.

Peter is appalled and says to the Lord that he never has nor would ever eat anything unholy and unclean. The voice says, "What God has cleansed, no longer consider unholy."

Peter is greatly perplexed about the vision. This is a devout Jew who understands that there is purpose in the law. God did not create the law arbitrarily. The law describes and displays God's righteousness. How could something God has designated unclean become clean?

Peter continues to ponder the vision, and while he reflects on it, men shows up at the door asking for Peter to go with them to see the centurion Cornelius. When Peter is told that God sent an angel to Cornelius, a Gentile, the light goes on for him.

Verse 28 is critical. Peter tells Cornelius and his household that it is unlawful for a Jew to associate with a foreigner or visit him. Yet Peter says that God showed him that he should not call ANY man unholy or unclean.

The point is this: what Peter realized is that no man should be considered unclean or unholy. When God said to Peter, "What God has cleansed, no longer consider unholy," He was telling Peter that He had made atonement for all men. He had not changed the law about what animals were edible!

Atonement is cleansing

This short statement from God to Peter—"What God has cleansed, no longer consider unholy"—sums up what Christ's death on the cross means to the whole world. His death was the atonement for all mankind. It satisfied the debt or the penalty for original sin.

It is also important to mention here that the law that Peter was talking about in Acts 10:28 in terms of associating with a foreigner is not found in the Torah anywhere. But we will discuss that later in this article.

Look at Leviticus 16:29–30. This chapter is all about the law of atonement. It is the definitive statute regarding the annual ritual for Israel to make atonement for the nation. It symbolically reconciled the nation to God. It also foreshadowed the perfect atonement that would be made by Christ for all of mankind (see Heb. 10:10–12).

> And this shall be a permanent statute for you: in the seventh month, on the tenth day of the month, you shall humble your souls, and not do any work, whether the native, or the alien who sojourns among you; for it is on this day that atonement shall be made for you to <u>cleanse</u> you; you shall be <u>clean from all your sins</u> before the Lord.

In other words, atonement is a cleansing! This is what God was telling Peter. Christ's death had atoned for the sin of all mankind. Peter realized that nothing had changed regarding what is good or bad to eat. God had not cleansed those things or made them suitable for eating! Jesus Christ atoned for or cleansed all men.

This does not mean that all people are saved. Christ's death paid for the sin of the world, but individually, we are justified by faith. Faith alone is what determines whether we become righteous in God's eyes. Christ's death, or atonement, is a gift for all men. It allows for justification for all men individually by faith (Rom. 5:11–18).

The point I am trying to make about Acts 10 is that nothing changed from God's perspective about what is good to eat. He used that vision to help Peter understand what God had cleansed or atoned for. God forced Peter's mind into a quandary so that when the men from Cornelius showed up, Peter would automatically understand.

Now I am not saying that we are still under the law. I am saying that what God laid out in the law as unclean to eat was still unclean or bad to eat. In other words, there was purpose behind God declaring certain things bad to eat. Nothing changed with that.

In Leviticus 11, God details which creatures can be eaten. At the end of the chapter, it says, "This is the law regarding the animal, and the bird, and every living thing that moves in the waters, and everything that swarms on the earth, to make a distinction between the unclean and the clean, and between the edible creature and the creature which is not to be eaten" (Lev. 11:46–47).

This explains why Peter was so perplexed. He could not understand how something that was bad to eat could suddenly become okay to eat. Then he figured it out when the representatives of Cornelius showed up.

While we have technology to protect from the hazards of certain unclean animals, there are still good reasons to avoid them. You can find the exhaustive list in Leviticus 11. Pork, shellfish, rabbits, and fish without scales like catfish are the usual suspects on American tables. You can do your own research on what is healthy and not.

Getting back to the law that Peter cited about associating with foreigners—it was a man-made law or tradition, not a law of God. In fact, if you go back through the books of Moses or the Torah, there are numerous passages that talk about welcoming the foreigners or aliens and being hospitable to them. Here are just a few.

> The stranger who resides with you shall be to you as the native among you, and you shall love him as yourself, for you were aliens in the land of Egypt; I am the LORD your God. (Lev. 19:24)

> There shall be one standard for you; it shall be for the stranger as well as the native, for I am the LORD your God. (Lev. 24:22)

> If an alien sojourns among you and observes the Passover to the LORD, according to the statute of the Passover and according to its ordinance, so he shall do; you shall have one statute, both for the alien and for the native of the land. (Num. 9:14)

> You shall not oppress a hired servant who is poor and needy, whether he is one of your countrymen or one of your aliens who is in your land in your towns. (Deut. 24:14)

And do not forget the one above that I quoted regarding the Day of Atonement, Leviticus 16:29–30.

God has always intended that Israel be a light to the nations. The Jews were never supposed to treat people with disdain. They were told not to intermingle in marriage or to follow other nations' gods, but if a non-Jew was seeking friendship, there was no law against it.

This tradition of the Jews to not associate with Gentiles was something concocted by corrupt religious leaders. Guess what? It is the same with the church. We are to be in the world but not of it. We are to be just as hospitable to nonbelievers as Israel was to be to non-Jews. But we are not to marry unbelievers. God is the same yesterday and today!

28
Your Faith Has Saved You

> And those who were reclining at the table with
> Him began to say to themselves, "Who is this
> man who even forgives sins?" And He said to the
> woman, "Your faith has saved you; go in peace."
> (Luke 7:49–50)

This is the story of the immoral woman who washed Jesus's feet and anointed Him with oil. Jesus told the people who were in the house of the Pharisee at the time that her sins had been forgiven, and it was her faith that accomplished it.

I wanted to include this chapter to specifically address the notion that we have no choice about our salvation, that God chooses some, and that those He chooses have no choice but to be saved. The rest have no choice but to be condemned. In other words, there is no free will when it comes to salvation. Most label this belief as Calvinism.

Jesus told the woman that her faith had saved her. Paul says in Ephesians 2:8 that we are saved by grace through faith. So which is it? Are we saved by faith or grace?

Both. Without grace, we cannot be saved; and without faith, we cannot be saved.

There is a two-way dynamic that takes place when a person is saved. First, God must draw the person to Him (John 12:32) and reveal Himself (Luke 10:22). Grace is given to an individual to understand the saving message of the gospel of salvation (Heb.

6:4–5). The person at that time has a choice to believe or reject that message.

Of course salvation can be a much more complicated and nuanced experience than the description above. It can take months or years for an individual to come to the realization or understanding of the truth as well as the humility to accept it.

But at some point, that individual will come to a critical moment where the decision is now or never, and God only knows that moment. I believe that is what Hebrews 6 explains.

Hebrews 6 is saying there is a point where a person is enlightened to the extent that they taste the heavenly gift of salvation and partake of the Holy Spirit. They have been brought to a place where they completely understand the truth and see the light, and they can either reject or accept it.

If they accept it, they are saved by their faith. Their faith justifies their salvation (Rom. 5:1), and it is the power of God's grace that seals them in the Holy Spirit (Eph. 1:13).

If they reject it, then they cannot be brought back to that point again. It is impossible to renew them again to repentance, says the writer of Hebrews.

It is implicit in these verses that if your faith saves you and if it is something that you can reject, then it is something you have free will about.

Jesus is clear when declaring to the woman, "Your faith has saved you." It was the woman's choice to believe in Jesus as her Savior. He did not say, "I have saved you." He could have, and it would have been accurate. But the fact that He told her that her faith saved her tells us that we have a say about whether we live forever or whether we are judged and destroyed.

Speaking of being judged, how can anyone be judged for their unbelief if they had no choice in not believing? How can anyone be guilty if they had no other option but to not believe?

Reformed theology, or Calvinism, teaches that everyone is born into condemnation, which is true. But they believe God then chooses some out of that condition without their consent, and the others will remain there and be judged. But you cannot be rendered guilty for something you have no choice about.

Referring to John 12:32, Jesus said that when He is "lifted up from the earth," He would "draw all men to Himself." Why would He say that He will draw all men to Himself if He is only going to choose certain ones for salvation? He would not. He "desires that all men be saved and come to the knowledge of the truth" (1 Tim. 2:4). Whom does Jesus choose? Everyone who chooses to believe in Him!

29
Never Means Never

One of the most repugnant positions that some churches embrace or even tolerate is the notion that a Christian can lose their salvation. It is the idea that if a professed Christian engages in grossly sinful behavior (which all sin is with God anyway) or stops living a public Christian life, then they either were not really saved in the first place (which certainly could be true) or they have walked away from God and forfeited their salvation.

The question is, is it even possible to lose one's salvation? To think or believe that you can lose it or have it taken away is not only unscriptural but also insulting to God. You are saying that God breaks His promises. There are many passages that I could cite to show that when you get saved, it is permanent no matter what you do. But I only want to look at two here.

The first is John 10:27–30: "My sheep hear My voice, and I know them, and they follow Me; and I give eternal life to them, and they shall never perish; and no one shall snatch them out of the Father's hand. I and the Father are one."

Jesus is making a clear and definitive statement. He says He knows who His sheep are, and He gives them eternal life. You cannot get more explicit than that. When you are given eternal life, that means you are going to live for eternity. Period. And that's exactly what Jesus says: "And they shall NEVER perish!" Never is never! No matter what—not no how, not no way (a wink to the cowardly lion)!

Anyone who believes and receives Christ as Savior will not be judged and thrown into the lake of fire and destroyed. That is the definition of perish (see the chapter "The Judgment"). Eternal life means you will live forever with the Lord.

It is not necessary, but the other verse that I want to include here is Romans 11:29: "For the gifts and calling of God are irrevocable."

Now I realize that the context for this passage is the promise to Israel that it will be saved after the fullness of the Gentiles has come in. It does not matter; it is still applicable. In fact, it demonstrates that the promise of eternal life is an unconditional guarantee.

God promised that He would send a deliverer from Zion and that He would remove Israel's sins. This was not dependent on Israel's performance or behavior. This was an unconditional promise to Israel just as the gift of eternal life is an unconditional promise to any person who receives it. Eternal life is a gift from God, and God says it is IRREVOCABLE!

This is a critically important, fundamental Bible doctrine. A believer, especially a new believer, needs to know that there is nothing that can change their relationship with God. There is no sin that can put them in jeopardy with the Lord. They can now obey God out of love and thankfulness rather than fear. Not only should this be the position a church stands on but it should also be taught.

30
The Real David and Goliath

I wanted to include this chapter because it demonstrates that you can press the Scriptures hard and it remains faithful to itself. I think this is an incredibly encouraging lesson.

I came across a video of a TED talk. A TED talk is a short lecture on a topic that is distributed freely by TED Conferences LLC. TED stands for technology, entertainment, and design. Their slogan is, "Ideas worth spreading."

The video I saw was by a gentleman named Malcolm Gladwell. You can google it. The title is "The Unheard Story of David and Goliath." He also wrote a book about his thoughts titled *David and Goliath: Underdogs, Misfits and the Art of Battling Giants*. I have not read the book, but I'm guessing Gladwell's TED talk is a CliffsNotes version of his book. The video has had 6.5 million views. That is a lot of views.

Here is my CliffsNotes version of the TED talk.

Gladwell began his talk by stating that the story of David and Goliath in the Bible had always bothered him. More precisely, he said the story "really obsessed" him. He said he thought he had understood the story, but the more he studied it, the more he realized that he really did not understand it.

Here is the setting: The Philistine army and the Israelite army were encamped on opposing slopes of mountains with a valley in between. For all intents, it was a stalemate because neither army wanted to attack the other. To do so, the attacking army would have to come down its own slope, cross the valley, and attack up the enemy's slope. It would likely be suicidal. So the armies languished in a standoff.

> Then Samuel took the horn of oil and anointed him in the midst of his brothers; and the Spirit of the Lord came mightily upon David from that day forward. (1 Sam. 16:13)

Enter David. A short time before the epic contest, David had been anointed king of Israel by Samuel, and Saul was told that he would lose the throne. David then gets chosen by Saul to play a harp to soothe his mind. God had sent an evil spirit to torment Saul after David was anointed. At the time of Goliath's challenge, Saul did not know of David's anointing.

While the armies were encamped, David was going back and forth from Saul to tend his flock of sheep. On one occasion, David arrived at the Israelite camp, and he heard Goliath taunting the Israelite army. David was the only one who stepped up to accept the giant's challenge.

According to Gladwell, there was a tradition in ancient warfare that when armies were at a standoff, they would sometimes have a champion from each army fight each other to determine the outcome.

In his talk, Gladwell explains that he had always believed that David was an underdog in this classic tale. What he says he discovered was that the opposite is true. These were his reasons:

David is a deadly expert with the sling. Gladwell says in his talk that the expert slingers of the time could hit their target at distances of two hundred yards. They could knock birds out of the air.

Goliath assumed that he would be fighting an Israelite in hand-to-hand combat. Goliath was an infantry soldier and was expecting another infantry soldier. Goliath was fully clothed in heavy armor and weapons while David was unencumbered.

Gladwell assumes that Goliath is an abnormally tall man due to a condition of giantism called acromegaly. This is the condition that Andre the Giant had. According to Gladwell, it is characterized by a pituitary tumor that causes the gland to overproduce. Symptoms include poor eyesight and poor mobility, not to mention abnormal height.

Gladwell cited a couple of verses to back up his contention that Goliath suffered from this condition. He said the text showed that Goliath had to be led down the mountain because he could not see very well. He said that Goliath could not see David very clearly until he was only a short distance from him. Gladwell also cited a verse where Goliath said to David, "Am I a dog that you would come to me with sticks?" (1 Sam. 17:45). David was only carrying one stick, so Gladwell assumed Goliath had impaired vision.

I believe the first contention about David's skill with a sling is correct. In Judges 20:16, it says the seven hundred choice slingers could "sling a stone at a hair and not miss." It is a deadly weapon, and David knows how to use it. My guess is that he probably ranks among the most proficient slingers of his day. No doubt he uses it often in protecting his sheep.

It is also true that David was at an advantage without the armor. He had no intention of battling Goliath with sword, shield, and spear—weapons Goliath brought to the fight. David was far nimbler without the armor and heavy weapons.

However, the Scriptures are clearly in opposition with Gladwell's third contention that Goliath is physically impaired. Gladwell is inserting things into the texts that are not there.

First, in 1 Samuel 17:41, it says that "the Philistine came on and approached David, with his shield bearer in front of him." I do not see anywhere in the text where you can deduce that he was being led by anyone as a seeing eye dog would lead. The shield bearer was doing what he was supposed to do: carry the shield! I would presume that he was in front because that was the formal way they did things. On a practical level, in the event Goliath had to quickly take the shield, he could do so without taking his eyes off his adversary.

Second, the Bible does not say that the Philistine was able to make out David ONLY when he got close to him. All it says in 1 Samuel 17:42 is that Goliath "looked and saw David."

You cannot conclude from that verse that Goliath had bad eyesight. In fact, in 1 Samuel 17:48, it says that "when Goliath rose and came and drew near to meet David, David ran quickly toward the battle line to meet Goliath." This indicates that they were still significantly far apart from each other when Goliath said what he did about the sticks.

As far as saying sticks (plural) instead of stick, that can easily be chalked up to a euphemism. David was only carrying one stick, it is true, but it is not enough to justify the assumption Goliath was hard of seeing.

Regarding Goliath's height, it was not a gland problem. He was from a race of giants. In 1 Chronicles 20:4–8, Scripture describes other fights with giants who were related to Goliath. In verse 8, it says they were all descended from the giants in Gath. In Hebrew, the word *giant* in these passages is *rapha*. It is the root of the word *Rephaim*.

The Rephaim were a race of giants. Scripture says that Og of Bashan, who was between thirteen and fourteen feet tall, was the last of the Rephaim. The giants of Gath, which included Goliath, were most undeniably descended from the Rephaim. It was not a case of human deformation. The Rephaim (which included the Emim and the Anakim [Deut. 2:11]) were descendants of the Nephilim from Genesis 6.

One last thing about Goliath: he was their CHAMPION! The Philistines would not have sent some slow-footed, nearsighted klutz to beat the Israelites' best! The Philistines would have sent an undefeated, veteran warrior!

Was David an underdog? Only in stature. David knew his skill level, but the most important thing that he knew was that God was with him and that God would deliver Goliath into his hand. Gladwell completely ignored this fact.

> This day the Lord will deliver you up into my hands, and I will strike you down and remove your head from you. And I will give the dead bodies of the army of the Philistines this day to the birds of the sky and the wild beasts of the earth, that all the earth may know that there is

a God in Israel, and that all this assembly may
know that the Lord does not deliver by sword or
by spear; for the battle is the Lord's and He will
give you into our hands. (1 Sam. 17:46–47)

David was a prophet, and his prophecy was fulfilled exactly as
he foretold. Remember the verse at the beginning of this article? It
says that the spirit of the Lord came upon David mightily from the
time of his anointing going forward.

If I may say something else about the idea of each army's champion fighting to settle a grudge, I believe it was much deeper than
just a fight. I believe the armies saw something much more profound
in the outcome. As far as the armies were concerned, it was a question of whose God/god was superior. Why else would the Philistines
run when Goliath was killed? They still held their high ground after
David killed the rapha. It still would have been physically daunting
for the Israelites to attack up the slope to the Philistine position.

The reason the Philistines ran was because they believed that
the God of Israel was going to crush them. Everyone on both sides
heard David declare what God was going to do. Remember, David
said "that all this assembly may know!"

After Goliath bellowed his trash talk, David loudly proclaimed
his prophecy. In the valley, his voice would have carried nicely up the
mountain slopes. The acoustics were ideal. It was a natural amphithe-
ater. And when it happened just as David had shouted, the Philistine
army scattered like cockroaches when the light goes on.

When David held up the decapitated head of Goliath, the
Philistines' hearts melted! It happened exactly as David had declared.
David was not an underdog. Goliath never had a chance. But it was
not because Goliath was physically impaired.

31
The Real Tower of Babel

> Come, let us build for ourselves a city, and a tower
> whose top will reach into heaven, and let us make
> for ourselves a name; lest we be scattered abroad
> over the face of the whole earth. (Gen. 11:4)

The story of the tower of Babel has always puzzled me. Why would God be concerned about a bunch of people building a structure high up into the sky? Usually the interpretation of the passage goes like this: The people wanted to build something that would reach up to the heavens where God was. God saw what they were doing and realized that the people were accomplishing the goal.

> Behold, they are one people, and they all have the
> same language. And this is what they began to
> do, and now nothing which they purpose to do
> will be impossible for them. (Gen. 11:6)

So God went down and confused their language and scattered them abroad from there over the face of the whole earth, and they stopped building the city. (Interesting that Scripture says they stopped building the city, not the tower. Make a note of this.)

The first problem with this explanation is that God would not care about someone trying to build a tower up to heaven other than that it would be an exercise in futility, and God is opposed to wasting time and money. God says in Jeremiah 31 that the "heavens cannot be measured." It is not possible to reach God's throne.

Obviously, God was not thinking about the tower reaching up to heaven where He is enthroned when He said, "Nothing which they purpose to do will be impossible for them." So let's break things down. What is going on here?

The first thing to address is who the people are. You must back up into the previous chapter. This is postflood, and chapter 10 chronicles all the generations of Noah's sons. It documents all the descendants of Noah leading up to the city of Babel in chapter 11.

In other words, the people of Babel were the entire human race up to that point after the flood. That is what chapter 10 verse 32 says: "These are the families of the sons of Noah, according to their genealogies, by their nations; and out of these the <u>nations were separated</u> on the earth after the flood."

Notice that the verse says they were separated into the nations (in case you missed the underline). Continuing into chapter 11 verse 1, it says, "Now, the whole earth used the same language." And in chapter 11 verse 6, it says that they are "one people."

What is happening in the story of Babel is an explanation of how and why the descendants of the sons of Noah were separated into the nations. What did God command Adam and Eve in the garden? "Be fruitful and multiply, and fill the earth, and subdue it" (Gen. 1:28).

And what did the people of Babel led by Nimrod say? "Let us make for ourselves a name; lest we be scattered abroad over the face of the whole earth."

What we see in this story is the people of earth defying God and His purpose for mankind. Instead of obeying God and representing Him, they are choosing to create their own identity and purpose and NOT be scattered over the earth and fulfill God's command. The tower was simply going to be the center of that identity. It would be the symbol of who they are. And it would be the focal point of their existence geographically—a sort of tether, if you will. According to the Book of Jubilees, the tower, at its peak, reached a height of 1.6 miles. That is 8,500 feet approximately!

Think of it this way: they wanted to stay together where they were, and the tower, which would have been the height of six empire state buildings, would be a visual hitching post. So as the population grew and spread, they could always see the tower and stay together. The tower would be the center of their civilization, and it would also be the center of their identity.

Remember I said to make a note of the fact that Scripture said they stopped building the city instead of the tower after God confused their language? I think that is just more evidence that the tower, in and of itself, was not the issue with God. The issue was that they were creating their own identity and purpose and ignoring God and His plan.

Man was created to image God, to represent His name. God came down and confused their language to scatter mankind over the earth and fulfill the commission He gave Adam and Eve. Nimrod, who led the people to build the tower, was an Antichrist type, just as his government was a foreshadowing of a coming world government.

A day is coming soon when another man will unite the world to make a name to follow other than the Most High God. But that also will fail, of course, and then the King of Kings will set up His kingdom that will last forever. Very soon (Heb. 10:37).

ABOUT THE AUTHOR

Daniel Baker is a financial adviser in Missouri. He has studied and taught Bible prophecy for twenty years as well as published numerous articles on the subject. His work has been read worldwide.

CPSIA information can be obtained
at www.ICGtesting.com
Printed in the USA
BVHW031907020421
604057BV00008B/155